David Davidson

**Thoughts on the Seasons**

David Davidson
**Thoughts on the Seasons**
ISBN/EAN: 9783337034504
Printed in Europe, USA, Canada, Australia, Japan
Cover: Foto ©ninafisch / pixelio.de

More available books at **www.hansebooks.com**

# THOUGHTS

## ON THE

# SEASONS, &c.

### PARTLY IN THE

## SCOTTISH DIALECT,

### BY

## DAVID DAVIDSON.

---

" *Verque novum stabat cinctum florente coronâ:*
" *Stabat nuda Æstas, et spicea serta gerebat:*
" *Stabat et Autumnus, calcatis sordidus uvis:*
" *Et glacialis Hyems, canos hirsuta capillos.*"—

OVID MET.

---

LONDON:
PRINTED FOR THE AUTHOR;
And sold by J. MURRAY, No. 32, Fleet-Street; and W. CREECH, Edinburgh.
MDCCLXXXIX.

THE

# PREFACE.

THOUGH the World should *laugh* in reading the following Sheets, I shall not *weep* because I have written them. But, I presume, it is only from my countrymen that the laugh can come, (for, surely, none will be fool enough to ridicule what he does not *fully* understand) and the satisfaction is but small in one Scotchman satyrizing another.—The same things please not all men.—'Tis as queer to be dissatisfied with another's way of writing, as it is to challenge him for having a *brown* beard,

because

becaufe his is a *black* one.—Every man in his humour—mine is obvious.—The Roman Senators had, their Auditors; the Stoick Philofophers, their Followers; and, why may not a Caledonian Bard be attended by, *his* Admirers? To deny him the privilege (at leaft the hope) would be barbarous.

While fome affect the path of fplendid life, others, lefs pleafed with *great* things, love to trace the fteps of the cottager; and, among woods, and rocks, and ftreams, admire the fcenes of Nature, undifguifed.

That I have expreffed my thoughts *partly* in my native dialect, was my inclination.

nation. Let not this inclination condemn the production; for, the *worth* of a ſtory conſiſts not merely in, the language in which it is told.

The chaſte, the harmonious Thomſon, when his proſpect extended but little beyond the walls of Kenſington Gardens, could circumvene the ſkirts of the Grampian Hills—there purſue the vagrant ram, from his fold to the mountain—conduct the bleating lamb from the hill, to its dam in the vale—view the finny race ſporting in the purling cryſtal ſtream—and, with the 'herd-boy, chaſe the fly-ſtung heifer, " low bellowing round the hills."

With

With a profpect, not more extenfive than Thomfon's, I have circumven'd the hillocks of my natal foil—mark'd the procefs of the acorn to the oak—attended the bee from the hive to the heathy hill—and followed the duckling from the egg to the ocean.

Throughout the whole, I have endeavoured to copy Nature.—Little, therefore, is farther neceffary by way of Preface, in defence of my Book; or, to keep it in countenance, if the unprejudiced admirers of Nature can find in it only, that the tale is not artful.

# SPRING.

HAIL, lovely Spring! thy bonny lyart face,
And head wi' plumrocks deck'd, befpeak the fun's
Return to blefs this ifle, and cheer her fprouts.—
Who can wi' fafety murmur at his lot,
Or *girn* at Providence, whom Heaven has fpar'd
Frae a' the weary wreck o' winter's wafte,
To keek at Spring?—Life lengthen'd is a gift.—
The torrent's fugh is hufh'd, the fpate is done—
The fwelled brook is dwindled to a burn.—
No wreaths o' fnow now on the hills are feen,
Nor, ba's like pyramids, upo' the plain.—
Soft-blowing winds diffolve the icy clods,
And cou'ters fhine behind the fturdy fteers.—
The little fecklefs bee, wi' pantry toom,
And hinny-crock ev'n wi' the laggin lick'd,

## SPRING.

Long looking for black Beltan's wind to blaw,
Drops frae his waxen cell upo' the ſtane—
The ſunny beams peep though his narrow porch,
Wi' ſklentin caſt—and wi' reviving pow'r
Beſtir his feeble joints.—In gladſome friſk
He eyes the bonny day—and, bizzing, tries
To trim his little wings, to walk, to fly.—
Now ſquintin at the ſun, he takes a ſten
Wi' ardent bir, and pitches on a ſtraw.
Then riſing hence, he wheels around the ſkep
To try his pith,—Syne, on the riggin lights—
Proud o' his growing ſtrength he bums on high;
And, ſkimming round, unto the brae he flies,
And lights upon a gowan—wi' his trunk
He ſcoops the yellow ſtore—refreſh'd at e'en
He, blythe returns wi' forage on his hips.—
His brother bees around him run in troops,
To prie the new-earn'd ſweets—and, farley a'
To ſee ſic gaucy thighs, ſic yellow bum.—
Induſtrious race! without or kirk or ſchool,

# SPRING.

Ye learn arts, and preach morality!—
Would men but learn frae you, wee winſome elves,
They'd be more frugal—leſs to knav'ry prone.—
Now frae their cribs the tarry gimmers trot,
And, ſpread around the faulds, to crop the blade
Of tender graſs, or thriving waly.—Some
Aſcend the hill—and, ſtraying far afield,
'Mong ſcroggy braes, or lonely rocky glens,
Seek out a lamming place.—Upo' the cliff
Within a hallow craig where none dare go,
The eagle has his haunt—a royal neſt—
Bequeath'd to him and his, ſince time unken'd—
There to the beetling rock he hefts his prey,
Of lam or hare, ta'en frae the vale below.
Upo' the brow he ſits, and, round him deals,
Unto his unfledg'd ſons, the fleſhy feaſt—
Himſelf wi' penches ſtaw'd, he dights his neb,
And to the ſun, in drowſy mood, ſpreads out
His boozy tail.—Right o'er the ſteep he leans,
When his well-pleniſh'd king-hood voiding needs;

## SPRING.

And, sploiting, strikes the stane his grany hit,
Wi' pistol screed, shot frae his gorlin doup.—
Now midway in the air the buzzard skims,
The staney dale, fu' gleg upon his prey.—
Wi' hungry maw he scoors frae knowe to knowe,
In hopes of food in mowdy, mouse, or streaw.—
As o'er the birny brae mayhap he wheels,
The linties cour wi' fear—and, frae his branch,
Whereon he sat and sang, the mavis pops
Into the thorny brake—his singing spoil'd.—
If chance upon an ash above the lin,
A hoody has her nest—on seeing the gled
Approach too near her bounds, down on the foe
She darts, wi' wicked skraich—syne, at his tail,
Frae 'mang the scroggs, the yorlins fly in cluds,
Like tykes upon a beggar.—Down the glen,
Far from the tread of any human foot,
Upon a blasted oak, the croaking ra'en,
Fell thief o' gosling brood, has his retreat.—
The cloken hen, when frae the kipple-sit

She

She breaks her tether, to the midden rins
Wi' a'her burds about her, fyking fain,
To fcrape for mauks—and little ducks and geefe
Rin todlin on the green, a' free frae fear,
Down in a han-clap comes the corby cock,
Upo' the middin tap, and, wi' a twirl
Snaps frae his mither's hip the fav'rite chick.—
Faft off he flies wi' burdie in his clutch,
Far 'hind unto his neft—and, 'fore his mate,
Lays, the delicious meltit—war's proclaim'd
Againft the corby race—and glens and heughs
Are hunted for the cockrel—but in vain.—
Meanwhile twa 'herds upo' the finny brae
Forgathering, ftraught down on tammocks clap
Their nether ends, and, talk their unco's o'er—
Auld farnyear ftories come athwart their minds,
Of bum-bee bykes, pet pyats, doos, and keaws,
An' a' the winfome fports that 'herds are prone to.—
While at their tauk fae thrang, upo' the bank
Juft at their feet, alights the corby craw,

## SPRING.

And frae his hillan the poor mowdy whups—
They mark the way he takes, when quick as *flint*,
Adown the darkfome glen he wheels, and, on
His aerie lights.—Rejoiced at the fight,
They brattle to the brow—whence, they defcry
Upon a blighted afh, above a pool,
The fum of prefent hopes—a plenifh'd neft.—
Straight down the fteep they flide wi' canny care,
Ilk at the other's en', frae ftump to ftane,
For fear o' donfy whirl into the ftream;
Syne, up ane fpeels, and, in the wooly haunt,
Wi' dizzy eyes, he views the fpreckled ftore.—
Forth frae the neft the warm treafure's drawn,
And, in his bonnet flung—hence homeward they
Poft, peghing, wi' their fpoil.—The pingle-pan
Is on the ingle fet—into the flood
Of firey frith the lyart gear is caft,
And addled eggs, and burdies without doups,
Play round, promifcuous, in the boiling pool,
A' ftiff'ning to a pafte by dint o' flame.—

Hence

# SPRING.

Hence in the neſt replac'd, the wa'fu ra'en
Muſt, ere ſhe *clock* them, travel to the eaſt,
Unto the *burn* that through auld Eden rins,
Where Adam and his Wife, as ſtory tells,
Did plant their bow-kail, and the garden delve;
And thence, fetch frae the brook, a yellow ſtane,
To chip the ſhell.—The ſun, bra honeſt light!
Now o'er the *lift* a larger circuit takes;
Gets ſooner out o' bed, goes later ly,
And, by his kindly pow'r upo' the riggs
Makes briers and dockens grow.—The farmer, ere
The cock had craw'd day, or the ducks had drate,
Upo' the hallan-ſtane, ca's frae his cot
The drowſy callan—wi' unwilling ſtep
He ſtalks the bent, wi' ſcarrow o' the moon,
To tend his *fleecy care*.—Upo' the glebe,
Soon as the day glents ruddy frae the Eaſt,
The ploughman ſtrides, and, frae his wauked loof
Flings forth the yellow grain, into the lap
O' th' fallow'd field.—The harrows yok'd, and, now,

## SPRING.

*Bawſy*, reluctant, tears the breckan roots
Harſh, ſpaul frae ſpaul, and ſhuts the ſawing ſcene.
Bright, dainty Heaven! " be gracious—now that man
Has done his part"—ye warm breezes blow!
Ye drizzling ſhow'rs decend! but frae the fields
May white fair-farren froſts keep far awa.—
Thou hot-fac'd ſun! who chears the drooping warld,
And gars the buntlins throſtle, by thy pow'r,
Look laughing frae thy ſky—and, with thy heat
Temper the ſcatter'd clods, and, ſouder all
Into the perfect year.—Nor gentles a'
Who live in pancake biggins, rich an' fine,
In bonny hinni'd fields, by whoſe door-ſtane
Braid ſtrans o' butter rin—who ne'er have felt
The ſting o' empty wyme, nor poverty,
" Think theſe loſt themes unworthy of your ear."
Sic ſangs as thae, the *heather headed* bard *
Of Scotland, ranted, as he trod the glebe;
And, Caledonia's taſte thought it nae ſhame
To croon the o'er-word.—Kings, time 'moſt forgot,

* Burns.                     Them-

## SPRING.

Themselves delighted wi' their taes to tread,
The fallow'd fur' behind the bended *share*.—
Bra healthfu' toil! well worth the care o' Kings.—
With thee, Dependance never had a place.—
Scepter'd hands may a' their power display;
And, dorty minds may luxury admire—
O'er sceptres sock! thou bearst the gree awa—
With thee, corruption is a fremmit name.—
" *Ye* generous Britons venerate the plough!"
And, let your braes frae, *Bass* to utmost *Thule*,
Wave wi' the *staves* of life, the wheaten stalks;
That, every needy pilgrim on his way,
May find support throughout the staney vale,
And, get a heezy o'er the sleugh o' *want*.—

Not o'er the corny riggs alone, the sun
Spreads forth his yellow rays—the benty brow
Nods wi' luxuriant heather, in whose skirts,
The churlin moor-cock woes his *valentine*,
Couring coyish to his sidelin tread.—

Up

Up the meand'ring stream the verdure rins,
And, lilies spread their foliage to the day.—
Rankly springs the rush around the pool,
And, saugh-trees blossom on ilk burn brae—
Unfolding by degrees their leafy stems,
The cat-tails whiten through the verdant bog.—
All-vivifying Nature does her work —
(Though flow, yet, sure) not like a racklefs coof
O' prentice wabster lad, who breaks his spool,
And, wastes the waft upo' a mis-rid purn;
But, like a mistress o' her trade, she weaves
Through stem and leaf, the vegetative pow'r;
Till, the fu' flow'red bank displays a fight
Of crawfoots, bowing wi' luxuriant nod.—

On banks like thae array'd, oft let me walk,
And, meditate on *Him* who cleads the yeard
Wi' sic bra flow'ry dress—and, who regards,
Wi' faithfu' care, the work o' faithless man.—
On banks like thae, amang the rising tribe

O'

O' Sprigs and Walys, *Contemplation* grows.—
There, *Meditation* springs up wi' the elm—
On's airy top aspires to Providence;
And, with the bri'r, creeps to him on the ground.—
Upo' the juicy bark now infects prey,
And, strive the embryo fruit i'th' bud to kill.—
These to destroy be't now thy watchfu' care.—
The sinny rays wide blinking on the wa'
In noon-day height, lead frae their winter cells
The sable race *o'clocks*—and, vernal warmths,
Descending, rouse, the pismires—and, from
His slimy hole entice, the capped snail—
Wight destructive! by thy eating power
The gard'ner's labor's lost, and, a' the hopes
O' plenty perishes beneath thy wyme.—
Black troops o' midges floating on the breeze,
To some warm nook repair, where calmness reigns;
And, there, wi' singing din, and frisky shanks,
Dance round the *bayes*, like pipers at a *wake*;
And, play their gambols in the sinny beams.—

Of

## SPRING.

Of thefe beware.—Faft o'er the verdant leaf
The *footy bitter* caft, or, midft the throng
O' infects hiv'd, pour forth the wat'ry death.—


'Twas in this infant feafon of the year,
When, ducks a paddock-hunting fcour the bog,
And, powheads fpartle in the oofy flofh;
That Donald, tir'd wi' lang-kail in a mun,
At's ain fire fide, long'd for the flipp'ry food,
And dainty cleading o' fome unken'd land.—
Long had he dream'd o' wealth and, riches bra,
In unco climes; but, frae his friends had kept
The winfome fecret.—On the hill-top he
Us'd oft' to walk, and, fighing, take farewell
O' a' the bonny glens, the finny braes,
And, nei'brin booricks, where he danc'd and fang—
Now loofing beauty in his wayward look.—
Oft downward to the Weft he'd watch the fun,
And, think within himfel—" If I could once
Reach, fafe, the fouthern fhore, to Mexico

Or

Or old Peru, among the diftant woods,
Where chiels wi' footy fkins, an' yill-caup een,
Hae their abodes—who routh o' riches fin',
Nought knowing of their worth—who for a knife

Or penny whiffle, will part wi' their gold
In gopinfu's—or, for a roofty nail

Will fwap their faireft gem."—On this he thought,
And, what he thought at day, at night he dream'd—
But, nor his dady nor his mither ken'd
The lad's intent—nor what great ftore o' wealth,
In fpeculation, he had hoarded up—
Till ae ftill e'en', as faft upo' his bed
The lad, in flumber wrap'd, tracing the vein
O' yellow ore through many dreamy fcenes,
Upftarting to his centre, mutter'd long,
In broken tone, the fubject o' his plan;
Which being o'erheard, his little titta Jean
Cries, " Dad, our Donald dreams!" fyne, by his tae
Takes hold—and, plain's my thum' he fays," *Peru.*"

## SPRING.

Moorland Willie and his wife
    Liv'd bienly near Strathboggy—
Nay ither way did they feed life
    Than, frae a timmer coggy—
Contented he, kind hearted she—
    Their plans did ever jingle—
And, not by any o'er the lea
    Were ever seen to pingle,
          'Bout straes, that day.—


While hale and fear, wi' his twa han's
    He kept the crowdy gawin—
And wad hae kemp'd wi' any man
    At dyking, or at mawing.—
Sae snug they liv'd on what they earn'd,
    That, nane were e'er mair happy—
And, when great folks at ither girn'd,
    *They* drown'd their care in nappy
          Fu' brown, that day.—

A son

## SPRING.

A fon they had whafe name was Gib,
 A lad o' muckle gumſheon—
Who cou'd rin o'er the Greek fu' glib,
 Or, count pints in a puncheon.—
Nae lad than he mair fpruce, in faith,
 At either kirk or market—
On's back a coat o' hame-made claith,
 And, underneath weel farket
     Wi' harn, that day.—


At fairs, aboon the countra lads,
 Gib held his head right canty—
Whoe'er did flight him gat a daud,
 Whenever he was ranty.—
The laſſes a' baith far and near,
 Lik'd Gibby o' the clachan—
Wi's bonnet trigg aboon his ear,
 An' face for maiſt part laughin
     Wi' joy, that day.—

## SPRING.

By moonlight led, upo' the green
    The chiels wad meet in daffin,
And warfle for a corkin preen;
    Syne, to the yill a' quaffin—
Gib's Dady aft wad claw his loof,
    An,' pinch, and pu' his jazy,
To fee ilk flegging witlefs coof,
    Get o'er his thum' a heezy
                  In fun, that night.—


Now Gib will leave his native land
    In fpite o' a' their banter—
What fignifis't on ftanes to ftand
    An' round the kail-yard faunter?
Shall I, fays Gib, ftay here a' hame
    Like witlefs Willy Clinted,
Whafe pladdin wafcoat o'er his wyme
    Shaws, he's in's porritch ftinted!
                  Sae toom, that day.—

                          Gib's

Gib's now gane for the Weſtern ſeas,
 Whare ſelchs an' pellucks whamble,
And's left his gear a' hame to theſe,
 Wha for't think worth to ſcramble.—
Frae's ain houſe en' unto the ſhore,
 He ſcoor'd wi' a' his mettle,
An' 's aft as aſk'd, Gib's anſwers were,
 " To Halifax to ſettle"
           In tred, that day.—


As on he trudg'd through Paiſley town,
 The wabſter lads kept glowrin—
But, Gibby's *een* were not his own,
 On leaving Meg Maclaurin—
He ran a wee, and ſyne, did ſtan'
 To ſee the burdies ſinging;
And, thought he heard as he was gawn,
 Strathboggy bell a ringing
           Wi' wae, that day.—

C   But

## SPRING.

But now the lad has ta'en the fea,
    An' weftlin, at a venture,—
He fcuds alang wi' heart as free,
    As 'prentice frae's indenture—
Although his Maggy on his mind,
    Did fometimes gie a dunner;
Yet, hopes that routh o' goud he'd fin'd
    O'er's love did come a lunner
              Right fell, that day.—


Auld Scotland foon was out of fight
    Through jaws an' billows roarin—
The fhip, fometimes, jump'd corbacks height,
    O'er whales afleep an' fnorin.—
Now, Gibby, cooft ae look behin',
    Wi' eyes wi' fainnefs blinkin,
To fpae the weather by the *fin*,
    But, coudna ftan' for kinkin
              *Rainbows*, that day.—

                  For

# SPRING.

For twice ten days clofe to the maft,
   Young Gibby fet his riggin—
Twa rafters kippled 'booh him faft,
   Serv'd for a better biggin.—
At length upo' the fhore he iten'd,
   And, flegg'd his highland fhankies,
But he by nane there, e'er was ken'd;
   Sae thick amang the Yankies,
          Queer chiels, that day.—


Gib now forgathering wi' the thrang,
   Met wi' his coufin Roger,—
Wha had na been, frae Glafgow lang,
   Till he became a Soger.—
Gib, too, enlifts—and hoifts up high
   A *whin-root* and a myrtle,
Syne, cluds draw near, with, on their thighs
   Swords made o' timmer fpurtles,
          To fight, that day.—

## SPRING.

Gib forward moved wi' the fun,
    Wi' a' his men in order,
Thinking to fright' wi' wooden guns,
    The whigs, frae 'bout their borders,—
But, phiz and crack, upo' the bent
    The whigs cam on in cluthers,
Wi' piftols' rair their lugs maift rent,
    An' put Gib in a fwither
                To rin, that day.—


The Yankies brattled down the brae,
    To fave themfels a bangin;
And, Gibby fkelp'd before the fae,
    Like Colly wi' a fhangin.—
Maift feck gaed hame, themfels, to tell
    The upfhot o' the bruilie;
But, fome wi' mair than powder fmell'd,
    Forfairn by the tweelie
                I'th breeks, that day.—

## SPRING.

For cowards some their craigs hadracks'd,
   And some they got a sneezin—
Gibby on them turn'd his back,
   Wi' a' his doup a bleezin *.
Sic was the fate o' norland Gib,
   Wha tarrow'd at his coggy—
When ither stammacks were fu' glib,
   An' guid, about Strathboggy,
               For brose, that day.—

    * Tar and Feathers,

# SPRING.

Now o'er the fields, the yellow goldfpinks fhow
Their blufhing *glory* to the warm breeze—
And, now, in dinfu bizzing, through the air
The bees crowd thick, to tafte the hinni'd fweets,
Upo' the broomy brae.—Fair to the fight
The whinny hill fpreads forth its yellow bloom;
And, heather-bells upo' the mountain's top
Wag wi' the morning dew.—Athwart the *fell*,
At dawn, fly Reynard fweeps the heathy brae,
Returning to his *hold* wi' reeking fnout,
Red in the flaughter o' his pilfer'd fpoil.—
Guilt goes not always free.—Frae hill to hill
Heard frae afar, the found of echoing horn
Advancing, fpeaks th' avenging hand comes on.—
The farmer rifing with the foaring lark,
Unto the mountain bends his early way,
To count his fleecy ftore.—Onward he goes,
Wi' bonnet o'er his haffet fklentin laid,
And, mind contemplative on *Him* who cleads
The yeard wi' verdure, and, kindly beftows

Bleffings

## SPRING.

Bleſſings on him, in fruitfu' goat or yowe.
Far in the ſilent nook o' buſhy glen,
Where none could ſee, trudging along, he ſpies
The luſtieſt wether o' his diſtant fold,
Bereft of life, and, by the ſpoiler torn.—
Amaz'd he ſtan's, an' wi' a waefu e'e
Beholds his *cypher* on his ſhorn ſide.—
Meanwhile, upo' the hill, the truſty pack
Loud opens on the track—the hunter's voice
Shrill-urging to the death, purſues amain;
And, down the buſhy vale, unto the ſpot
Of ſlaughter, *dogs* the foe.—Encourag'd by
The ſight o' bloody carcaſe, hopes ariſe,
That, the fell murd'rer is not diſtant far.—
The hunt renew'd—o'er dykes and birny fells
They ſcour upo' the ſcent—an', by an' by,
Advancing ſtraight on the expanded plain,
They preſs upo' their prey.—Arouſed by
The ſound of hound and horn, the *village* ſwarms
Upo' the bent.—Faſt frae their ſpinning-wheels

# SPRING.

Ilk hizzy fcours the bog—and, luckies, leal,
Rin toddlin to the knowe wi' rock in han',
To lend a lunner at the wily thief.—
Tir'd out wi' toil, at length poor Reynard finks,
Amidſt triumphant yells—and, to the bites
O' the devouring pack, without a youl,
Submits—The lovely May now uſhers in—
The hauthorn *ſhoots*, and o'er the buſhy dell
Each branch difplays exiſtence—on the hills
A' things look canty.—Shepherds, gay, begin
To big their booricks on each finny brae.
Frae hill to hill, through glens and ſtaney dales,
In fearch o' vagrant tips auld *bawty* rins—
While, up the ſteep, the 'herd wi' akin ſhanks
Purfues the fremmit yowe; and, now and then,
Erts on the tir'd tyke with " *ſheep awa a a !*"

Now, on the plain the lambs, at fetting fun,
Forſake their mithers and together meet,
Intent on mirth—to friendſhip having fworn—

        Ane

Ane taks a ſten, acroſs the foggy fur',
Wi' rackleſs force, ſyne, at his heels, in troops
The reſt rin brattlin after, kir and crouſe
Like couts an' fillies ſtarting frae a poſt—
Upo' a turf-dyke, ſtraught, they take their ſtan'
Or, round a tammock wheel, an', fleggin, toſs
The moudy-hillan to the air in ſtoor.—
The mavis now, upo' the buſhy bank,
Unto the trees emits his evening ſong;
And, a' around is peacefu' harmony.
Forth frae the whinny brae the maukin ſteals,
Wi' hirplin ſtep, down to the vale below,
To taſte the ſpringing wheat, or barley braird.
Wi' cautious care puſs doubles on her track,
An', tents the mavis' whiſtle at ilk ſten.
Cloſe to the *fur'* ſhe lays her downy wyme,
An', mumps the verdant blade wi' lonely fear.
Poor timorous elf! bane o' the farmer's toil!
In feeding here, thou only tak'ſt the tythe
For Nature's vicar—given, ſo to give—

         But

But fhould fome ruftic hallion fee thee here,
In thy luxuriant paftime, tent him well—
Againft thy life he lays the noofing grin,
Of hair, well twifted, frae the filly's tail.
Or, fhould the guid-man's fon, a racklefs chiel
As ever fitted fur' ahint the plew,
Come o'er the hill to count his outlar queys,
An', fee the hap frae ftauk to ftauk, thy life's
Not worth a whiffle,—Straught out o'er the bent
Hameward he fcours, we' a' his fpirits up;
An', frae the flake, aboon the ingle-en',
He whips the carabine.—The motion-hole
Frae ruft unfpik'd, and flint a flafhing fet,
Adown the bank he haftens, to the fpot
Where a' the treafure o''s uplifted hopes
Was feen to hirple—priming as he rins.
Frae bufh to bufh, afklent the bank he fcours;
(His cutes ilk ither fmite 'tween fear and joy)
Advanced near, he flings his bonnet by;
And, on his knees, creeps foftly to the hedge.

Poor

Poor hairy-footed thing! undreaming thou
Of this ill-fated hour, doft bienly lie,
And, chew thy cud, among the wheaten ftore.
Thy murdrer undifcover'd is prepar'd!
Now, through the wattled ftakes wi' glentin look,
He peeps upo' his prey, tho' dimly feen
Through wat'ry floods of joy,—and, cocking, takes
An enlang aim, to hit baith lugs an' tail.
His piece prefented—to the back he draws
The roofty trigger—and, as quick as thought,
In awfu' fplutter frae its riftin gab,
He ftrikes a ftane, fax ells ayont his aim.
The hills reverberate the dinfome yell.
Rous'd by the rumblin noife, poor maukin takes
The bent, wi' nimble foot—and, fcudding, cocks
Her bun, in rude defiance of his pow'r.
But, vengeance ever *dogs* and follows guilt.
The halloo rais'd—forth frae the ha'-houfe fwarm,
A pack o' yelpin tykes.—The cotter's cur,
At's ain fire-fide, rous'd by the glad alarm,
          Out

Out o'er the porritch-pingle takes a ften,
Laying the brofy weans upo' the floor
Wi' donfy heght, and, rins unto the bent.
O'er moor an' dale faft flee the yelpin tribe,
Encourag'd to the fcent by long halloos.
Some this way take the hill, the neareft cut,
Unto the place where laft the hare was feen—
Upo' the fcent fome round the valleys run,
The fartheft way—one fingles out a fheep,
Another fenfelefs cur purfues a crow.
Tir'd wi' the chace—ilk proud o' what he 'as done,
Now, homeward turns, and, o'er the burn brae
Streeks out his weary fhanks, and, laps his fill.


Far on the South, black fwelled clouds appear,
And, by degrees, athwart the lifted fky
Spread forth their gloom.—Now, low upo' the hil
The mift, recumbent, fpeaks a wat'ry day,
And, fhow'rs, refrefhing, to the bladed grain.
Down fa' the pearly drops, fucceffive; and,

Burns

## SPRING.

Burns out o'er their banks to rivers fwell,
Sweeping the verdant plain.—When ebb'd away,
But, not till then, an' when the billowy foam,
Borne by the ftream, wheels round the pebbled pool,
Then is the time, wi' gaudy-winged fly,
" To tempt the trout"—of afh well fplit and dri'd
Thy rod attach—and, frae the hoary fteed
Intwift, in even links, the lengthen'd line.
Thy gear prepar'd, now, up the ftream with care,
Trail the delufive infect—fometimes crofs
The whirlin eddy, where the ftream recoils
In eafy circling, to the oofy rock.
Ahint a ftane, clofe by the circling flood,
The moor-burn fpeckled king has his abode,
To catch what fidelin fa's adown the pool.
For him thy fkill exert.—Watch well the time
When floating clouds obfcure the glaring fun,
And o'er the ftream diffufe a gurly caft;
That inftant, on the pool extend thy line,
Wi' gentle fweep,—and bending by degrees

The

## SPRING.

The pliant rod, flow moving to the wind,
Lead on the gilded cheat—the well bufk'd hook,
Like animated infect in its pride,
Stately fkimming o'er the liquid flood—
Croffing his haunt, forth frae his pebbled bed
The fpreckled chieftain *draws*.—With eager grafp
He darts upon his death—fyne, on the bank
The yellow captive's flung, a fpartlin fight.
Be thus thy fport—but, let not on thy hook,
" The little captive ever torture meet."
When nw againft the fhallow, purling, ftream,
The Sa'mon fry, in troops a' bick'rin prefs,
And fhow their filver'd breafties in the glade,
On them have pity—tempt not, any way,
That fecklefs race; it is not worth thy care.
O! fpare the finny infants, when thou may'ft
With equal eafe, and, greater pleafure, lure
Their granam dads.—Now, frae the pebbled rill
Trace down the winding vale, unto the flood
Of rolling waters, in whofe gurgling ftreams

The

# SPRING.

The Sa'mon has his haunt.—Forth, at the dawn,
Wi' a' thy tackle trimm'd, take thou thy way
To where the lufty tenant o' the floods
Has, yaupifh, ta'en his ftan' in queft of food.
Now is the time, when on its filent banks
None has as yet, along the river trod,
To lure the monarch of thofe larger ftreams.
T'' infure fuccefs, mark well the water's hue—
If dark and moffy, of the lighter *caft*
Muft be thy fiy—if o'er a pebbled bed
The liquid current rolls, ferene and clear,
Then, frame thy infect of a darker tinge—
For, tent ye this, light laid on darknefs doth,
As darknefs does on light, the guile affift.
Athwart the ftream now fling the lengthen'd line,
An', mark wi' watchfu' e'e the fpringing game.
Should now, amidft the purling, foaming pool,
The wakefu' fifh efpy the glittering fly,
From Nature drefs'd, fkimming the cryftal flood,
Forthwith amain he plunges on his prey,

Wi'

## SPRING.

Wi' eager fwafh,—the lucky moment watch,
An', in his gills engorge the barbed death—
Syne gie him tether.—From the deep he turns
An' wi' the current drives—fometimes he fprings
Above the current's furface—and, fometimes,
Tries to take fhelter in the oofy bank—
Tir'd out with many turnings, to the flood
He lays his redden'd fide, and, gafpin, dies—
Syne round him flock, in troops, the fpirley race—
And, minnows frifk, now, that their foe is dead,
And, caper for the kingdom of the pool.

Oft in the ftreams of Dee, of old, I've feen
Sic fportive fcenes as thae, while on its banks
I trod, in heedfu' ftep, whipping the flood
To lighten care, and, chace the loit'ring fun
Wi' nimbler ftride, adown the Weftern fky.

Bra Dee! be thou my theme—Black frae the hills
That circumvene the fkirts of Craigenyell,

Thy

## SPRING.

Thy waters, in meand'ring currents run,
'Mong rocks and heather, many a weary mile,
Till, thou, connecting with thy sister-streams;
The river Ken, kissing the kindred flood;
Ye roll, in cudlin purlings to the sea.
How social on thy banks sits merriment,
Surrounded by the band o' laughing life!
Wi' leal rusticity I'd rather dwell
Above thy braes, than tread the gaudy courts
Of polish'd knavery, wi' a' the glare,
And tinsel'd dress, o' superficial greatness.

How rudely on the sight, seen frae afar,
Stand the unbatter'd walls of castle Trief!
Long hast thou, noble biggin! stood the bite
Of eating time, with harden'd front—and o'er
Thy nettl'd brow, the howling wind and storm
In vain keep whizzing.—In discordant times,
Thou hadst thy basis founded by the stream,
To guard thy isle, and, keep the thrawart chiels

Of nee'brin booricks, in fubmiffive awe.
Juftice and Humanity forgathering now,
(Striking the thumbs of friendfhip, ne'er to part)
An' flogging Tyranny acrofs the fea,
Have render'd thee, wi' a' thy ftately look,
Not worth a flea—thy tow'rs but ferve the turn
Of keaws and hoolets, where to fit and cry.

O fam'd

O fam'd an' celebrated caftle!
Before thou waft there was a buftle,
Wha wad be chief, and give the whuffle
                              In high comman'
An', tak a man's gun by the muffle,
                              An', gar him ftan.


Twa brithers then o' fpunky mettle,
At crowdy quarrel'd for, the kettle—
(Their mither beg'd they would it fettle)
                              Baith wi' a brainge
Sprang, hap an' ften, out o'er a nettle
                              An', cry'd, revenge.


Ilk faying the ither had affrunted—
Forth frae the houfe away they runted—
Swearing, their wroth could ne'er be blunted
                              While liv'd a clan.
That, would wi' gun or braid-fword dunt it,
                              Wi' man to man.

Wi' back to back on ane anither,
Towards ilk pole did walk a brither—
The younger loth to, leave his mither
     In wae an' grief,
Trav'ling along, clap'd in a fwither,
     His doup on Trief.


The rumour fpreading round the lochan,
The caufe could not be told for laughin,
How brithers pingled at their brochan,
     And made a din—
Ilk chiel fcrew'd up his dogfkin fpleuchan,
     An' aff did rin.


To Trief they march'd fu' blythe an' nimble;
Coblers wi' awls, an' wrights wi' wimbles;
An' taylors, fain the gear to thrimmle
     Of coward coofs,
Made powder-meafures o' their thimbles
     To fca'd their loofs.
       They

## SPRING.

They look'd upo' their new plantation—
It met the general approbation—
To guard it, each man, in his station,
     Wi' spade an' pike,
Through truffs an' stanes sought a foundation,
     To build a dyke.


Sae far secure, and, safe frae bullet—
To make a passage o'er the gullet,
Ilk on his shou'der flung his wallet,
     Wi' twa three stanes;
An' made a brig that ane could pull it,
     Nor, stress his banes.


They niest a' met to make a biggin,
Which, should above the clouds its riggin
Lift fair an' high.—Each wi' a piggin,
     Of pitch an' lint,
An' eggs, which he had got by thiggin,
     Made a cement.

On Kelton Hill there liv'd twa witches,
Who, feeing fic wark, out o'er the ditches

Frifk'd, nimbly, and, within their clutches
      Embrac'd Maclan;
An' told him, as he ftrok'd their mutches,
      *He* was the man.


As round the wa's the kimmers happed,
The broomfticks on their riggins flapped;
An,' now and then, their hurdies tapped,
      To raife the Deil,
Wha faid, he'd noofly crown the tap o"t,
      Wi' ftanes frae Screel.


The Die'l being naething but a cowan,
To make him free o' plumb an' trowan,
They gather a' about a gowan;
      An', o'er a fword,
Setting his auld black bum a lowin,
      Gave him the *word*.

         Upo'

Upo' the wa's a' han's then munted—
The *luckies* their tobacco lunted—
An' leugh to hear, the *auld boy* grunted
      Upo' the road,
As frae the hills he hameward runted,
      Wi' knowes o' sod.


In sweat and fun how they did jicker!
The 'prentice lads brought stoups o' licker,
Which, made their han's a' bra an' sicker,
      To ply the *mell*—
The De'il had brandy in a bicker,
      Out by himsel.'


Now through the air the *auld boy* birl'd,
To fetch mae stanes, wi's apron furl'd;
An', as he hameward with them whirl'd
      Frae auld Bengairn,
The string did break, an' down they hurl'd
      Into a cairn.

'Twas

'Twas a misfortune—but, to mend it,
He to Bentudor quickly ften'd it,
An' grafp'd the hill, but cou'dna bend it,
    It was fae dour,
Then, quoth he, " I'll wi' brimftone rend it,
    As fma as ftoor!"


Then down he fat, like ony mumper;
His hat threw by, pu'd out his jumper;
The kimmers cry'd, " O fic a thumper,
    Without a joint!"
An', as they fwigg'd the other bumper,
    Praifed its point.


But, while he thump'd the hill wi' peftle,
His brither mafons on the Caftle,
Call'd frae the wa's, wi, muckle buftle,
    For lime an' ftanes—
There was nane there to fill a mufflc—
    The De'il was gane!
     Like

Like 'prentice boy, that coud na help it,
Hame frae his wark awa he skelped,—
The little *furies* at him yelped,
                To see him puff;
And, Cerberus, though but just *whelped*,
                Did stan' an' yuff.


Nae mair behadden to sic swankies,
As, deil or witches, for their prankies,
The mason lads, wi' nimble shankies
                Hap'd frae the roof;
An', up, aloft, the timmer plankies
                Hove with their loof.

# SPRING.

Now frae the purling flood, an' diſtant vale,
Thy eyes ca' back, an,' o'er the verdant mead,
Behold the bluſhing profpect.—Who can paint
A waly-fprig like Nature?—Can the mind,
Wi' a' its pow'r and cunning, find a plan
To rival Nature wi' creative art?—
If wild Imagination cannot brag
Of hues like her's—if Fancy in the taſk
Fails and gives up—" Ah! tell me where I may
Find language to exprefs, the varied fcene?"
Behold the garden rich wi' herbs and flow'rs,
Opens its beauty to the wand'ring eye!
There, plenty rifes at the delver's heels,
An' fpeaks induſtry.—In the cool retreat,
By faugh an' boortree twining other's arms,
The humming bee refts on the honied bloom,
An,' lades his ſhankies wi' the yellow wax.
Down frae the fcra-built ſhed the fwallows pop,
Wi' lazy flaughter, on the gutter dub.—
Ane picks up ſtraes, anither, wi' his neb

## SPRING.

Works up the mortar.—On their tasks intent,
Ilk in his office plys, wi' heedfu' care,
Till, to the bauk depends the finish'd house.—
High on the sklentin skew, or thatched eave,
The sparrow, nibbling ravager o' garden pride,
Seeks out a dwelling-place.—Adown the grove,
The gouk, returned frae his foreign nest,
Haps, silent wi' his mate, frae tree to tree—
The infant year has not yet gien him strength,
To sing his old song—through his rusty throat.
He, hoarsely, tells the birds that he is come;
An' hostin, asks their leave to let him stay.


Should you, now, wander through the forest wild,
Amidst the leafy wilderness, there, in the claff
O' branchy oak, far frae the tread o' man,
The ring-dove has her nest—unsocial bird!
To woods and wilds her cooing cry she makes;
And, rocks, responsive, echo back her moan.
But, should you traverse the fair finny plain,

         Where,

# SPRING.

Where, now, the pied napple rankly grows,
An,' winnleſtraes excel the grov'ling fog;
There, to the ſkies the ſoaring lark aſpires,
Chants forth his airy notes unto the clouds;
While, far beneath his wing, his mate, ſecure,
Upo' her tammock ſits, and, gayly, fykes
To feel his neb, an' join his melody.
The thriving year, all ſocial an' ſerene,
Excites the feather'd-nation into love,—
Nor leſs, now, does the rougher brutal *world*
Feel, the enliv'ning power of the Spring.
The Bull, wi' curled front, and ſinews ſtrong,
Diſdaining th' keeper's voice, to pleaſure looſe,
Strays frae his herd, regardleſs o' his food,
An' ſcours, wi' furious flame, the diſtant vale.
There, ſhould obſtruction frae a neighb'ring king
His fierce deſire baulk, againſt the foe
Wi' a' the fury o' incenſed ſtrength,
The bellowing war commences.—Firſt, afar
The rowt is loudly heard, which, by degrees,

Approach-

# SPRING.

Approaching nearer, dwindles to a croon.
The rival now in fight, forth frae the herd
The foe advances, mutt'ring blood and death.
" Their eyes flash fury"—fidelin to the fight
They both come on, and, groaning in their might,
Make fan' an' pebbles, frae the hollow earth
Fly, whizzing in the air.—The 'herd-boy feeing,
Th' impetuous onfet, fearfu' o' the fray,
Flings plaid, an' luggy by, and, ftens the burn
Unto an aged elm, whence, out o' harm,
He views the warfle—laughing wi' himfel
At feeing auld *brawny* glowr, and, fhake his nools—
Dares him in fight, 'gainft any fremmit bill.
Snuffing and crooning done—the combatants
Butting in wroth, meet, furious, front to front,
And, " wi' impetuous force, the battle mix."
The fpanky heifers, breathing balmy round,
*Egg* on their fury, and their rage provoke.

 Thus, in the firey fteed, whofe blood is warm'd
By fpring's impulfive heat—the growing pow'r
       Diffufing

## SPRING.

Diffusing through his veins, the reign he scorns,
The thong defies, an,' o'er the verdant plain,
Exulting prances wi' unbridled mane.—


While these, in lusty strength, enjoy their loves,
The *saig*, poor dowy beast! nae pleasure kens
Aboon a gowan tap—for sovereignty
Or pow'r among the herd, he ne'er contends;
Nor, tweelies for the kingdom of the *loan*.
Shame fa' the ruthless han' that did thee wrong,
Or, durst wi' Nature meddle, to deprive
Thee of her bounty.—'Midst the wanton herd
Thou grazest, unsusceptible of passion's pow'r—
Like poor Italian piper, douf and dry,
Thou rangest o'er thy food, among the queys,
A' fearless o' thy *moo*, or cap'ring tail.
Unto thy smooth'ning tongue they fainly turn
Their yeuky rumps, and, sidelin bend their necks,
To catch thy friendly scart.—Between thy horns,
The cuddochs, wantonly, the battle feign,

And,

# SPRING.

And, ilk yaul-cuted heifer round thee playing,
In merriment, toffing her glaiket head
Beneath thy wyme, licks down thy boozy lifk;
And, rubs thy *courage-bag*, now's toom's a whuffle.
Thus, to the Spring awake, the brutal *world*
Feels the fu' pow'r o' the reviving year.—
Nor, of the chearing months, is human-kind
Lefs fenfible.—The modeft, virgin-blufh
Diffufes luftre on the beauteous maid—
And, robuft youths, whofe hearts for joy are form'd,
Now feel the impulfe of congenial love.
Unto the focial paffions form'd, Sufanna! come,
Pride of my fcanty verfe! come, and, hence, view
The winding valley, lavifh with its ftores.
See how the lily fips the purling ftream,
An,' o'er the bank in fcatter'd beauty, fpreads
The gay profufion! Yonder let us walk—
An' as we trace the windings o' the rill,
In blifsfu' talk, let paffion, leal and pure,
Direct our fteps.—Not a' the eaftern world

Can

Can boaſt of beauty, like the bluſhing face
Of *Virtue*, ſhining through the golden beams
Of *Modeſty*—and, breathing gales of *joy*.
Upo' the raviſh'd ſoul, wi' ſicker fit,
Truth treads triumphant—Nature's lovely gifts
In her improv'd by, undiſguiſed art,
Spread forth their luſtre to the riſing day;
And, with her, all is harmony and love.


I.

When fields grew green, and walys ſpread
    Their bloſſoms on ilk brae,
An' toddlin lammies o'er the lawn
    Did, daftly friſk an' play—
Auld *Brawny* wha in winter's cauld
    Had mourn'd for lack o' hay,
Seeking the blade of tender graſs,
    Far up the burn did ſtray.

For-

## SPRING.

### II.

Forgathering wi' the neighb'ring herd,
    A crooning, ſtraught, began,
Ilk cuddoch billying o'er the green,
    Againſt auld crummy ran—
The unco brute much dunching dried,
    Frae twa-year-alls and ſtirks,
But Jock the bill diſpers'd the tribe—
    He ſmell'd her moo and ſmirk'd.

### III.

Nae twa were ever ſeen mair thick
    Than brawny an' the bill;
An' when ſhe hameward took her way,
    He ſaw her o'er the hill—
Now brawny aft wad leave the craft,
    An' wander by herſel'
Cropping the blade upo' the ſtream,
    To where ſhe lov'd ſae well.—

## IV.

The cow was miffed at the flap,
  At milking time at e'en'—
The guid-dame, rinning to the herd,
  Spear'd whar fhe laft was feen—
" Upo' the hill" the callan cries—
  She cock'd her gaucy runt,
An' to Strathfallan green burn-brae
  Fu' nimbly fhe did ftrunt.—

## V.

The guid-dame fhe had ance been wed
  As weel as weel could be—
Now John forgot!—the beams of love
  Again, blink'd in her e'e—
Upon Strathfallan fhe had caft
  Lang time a wifhfu' leer,
But, coudna by her looks alone,
  The chiel's intention fpeer.

Ae

## VI.

Ae day Strathfallen took the bent,
  To hunt the fremmit yowes,
An' spying an unco, crummet, beaſt,
  Amang his broomy knowes;
He erted colly down the brae,
  An' bade him ſcour the flats;
But when the tyke to brawny came
  Down on his tail he ſat.—

## VII.

Nae dog Strathfallan could bring out
  Would e'er at brawny girn—
When ither kye gaed to the loan,
  Auld brawny croſs'd the burn.—
Now weir an' fence o' wattl'd rice,
  The hained fields incloſe,
Poor brawny preſſes 'gainſt the *thorn*
  But, cannot reach the *roſe*.

## VIII.

On this side stood the lonesome she,
    On t'other side her joe;
An', aye they stood, an', aye they mourn'd
    In dolefu', rowtin woe—
Lang had the twa at setting sun
    Upo' the fenced doon,
Their mutual sorrows interchang'd,
    By mony a weary croon.

## IX.

Dame Elspith, wi' attentive ear,
    Lang heard their loving yearn,
Strathfallan was before her e'e
    Her heart was 'yont the cairn—
Ilk rowt the twa gave thwart the burn
    Cam o'er her heart a dunt—
Strathfallan was as douf to love
    As, an auld cabbage runt.

### X.

At length, however, o'er his mind
 Love took a donſy ſwirl,
An' the fu' pow'r o' Elſpith's charms
 Gied his poor ſaul a ſkirl—
Strathfallen pitied brawny's croon,
 As, Elſpith did the bill's—
They brak the fence wi' leal conſent,
 An' let them hae their fills.

Still while I sing of Nature, let my thoughts
Pervade the wide domain, and, trace the *cause*
That, caused, causes, through the mighty *whole*.
Pure *Serenity* attaches to her side,
The wand'ring thought—and, *Contemplation*, still
Leads on frae work to work, creating, *Love*
An' *Admiration* in th' unbounded soul.
This is the noblest study of the mind—
It warms the bosom wi' the purest heat;
And, lifts the soul on rapt'rous, blisfu', wings,
To view the beauties of a happier world.

SUMMER.

# SUMMER.

SPRING turns away her sonsy, blushing face,
   Frae the refulgent glowr o' summer's sun,
Who comes athwart the sky wi' ardent look,
An' scorching pith, o'er burdies, beasts, and men,
Hence frae my auld clay-biggin let me gang,
Far up the woodlands wild, where, scarce a leaf
Bobs wi' the e'ening breeze—where cool retreats,
In caves and, spreading oaks, can shield my Muse
Frae the prevailing sun—where, not a ray
Of ardent heat may, spoil my whissle-pipe,
Or, cause my singing-keg to cast a gird.
There let me sit an' sing the leave-lang day,
An' chant the glories o' the circling year.
Or, let me, rather, on the heathy hill,
Far frae the busy world, whereon ne'er stood
A cottage, walk, an' churm my Lallan lays,

In hamefpun cleading, to the hollow rocks;
Thy top o' Screel! up in the midway air,
Lifts ftately to the fight—thy birny brow
Majeftic, frowns upo' the neighb'ring fells,
An' grov'ling hillocks o' the vale below—
Come Mufe! thou donfy limmer, who doft laugh
An' claw thy hough at, bungling Poets—come,
An' o'er my Genius crack thy knotted thong,
That my old reftive filly may go on
Wi' nimbler foot.—Brave Caledonians all
Attend, my rural fong; an' if ye're pleas'd
Wi' what I fing, let me your pleafure fee,
By ftooping to my theme.—The morning-ftar
Loofing its luftre, by the coming day,
Now twinkles, faintly, down the weftern fky—
An', through the world the gloomy robe of night
Begins to lofe, its, dreary, fable, hue.—

Hail to the Power that, in creative might
Ordain'd thefe twinkling orbs at firft to fhine!
With what an over-ruling, fkilfu', hand,

Were

Were these bright, rolling, planets form'd at first;
And, in the concave heaven, all glorious, plac'd,
To rule the varied hours !—How great the *Hand*
That cou'd the world's, unweildly, pond'rous, mass,
Create frae nought—and, in the ambient air,
For ages fix, an' bid it therein roll !
Let, now, Reflection view, the amazing whole,
And, tell the glories o' the vast domain.
The silent gloom is by the dawn outdone;
And, to their haunts the prowling beasts of prey,
Which, other regions breed, an' nourish up,
Scour nimbly.—Frae his bed o' ease
And sloth, luxurious *man* has not yet risen,
To bless the coming day.—Few joys can charm
*His* heart who, to the dead realm o' sleep
Commits the fleeting moments o' his life;
Or, in distemper'd scenes of vanity,
Extinguishes the powers o' his soul.

 The blue ey'd dawn springs frae the eastern clime
Wi' azure mantle ; and, the silent night,
Dusky

## SUMMER.

Dusky and gray, sinks 'yond the western main.
Hence, o'er the *lift*, the ruddy morn appears,
Scattering the misty clouds; and, wi' her broom,
Of radiant birch, sweeping the dew away.
Now infant Day, like chuffy-cheeked wean,
Peeps frae Aurora's bed, an' wi' a glowr
Makes hills, an' dales, an' valleys, brighten wide.
The darksome dell, the mountain's low'ring top,
The shady cavern, and, the dripping rock,
Swell, on the sight; and, wi' the early dawn,
Display, their awfu' beauties, blushing, wild.
Far up the winding vale, among the hills,
The mist floats, dusky, o'er the purling stream;
While, through the smoaking zephyr's wide domain,
The current's murm'ring noise is heard afar.
Fair o'er the fields the rising rays diffuse,
Their ruddy pow'r—an', frae the barley field
The maukin hirples, fearfu' o' the blade
Her trembling foot has mov'd—while on the brake
The mavis takes his stan', to hail the morn,

An'

An' chant his gratitude.—The pliant foot
Of early paffenger, athwart the vale,
Dunting, oppreffive, on the verdant path,
Beftirs the tenants o' the leafy brae.
The chanted matins o' the feather'd choir,
An', native voice of joy throughout the fields,
Provoke to harmony—and, all around
The woodlands wild is, peacefu' humming love.
Stir'd by the wakefu' note o' chanticleer,
The 'herd-boy o'er his fhou'der flings his plaid;
His broach an' luggy danglin by his fide;
An', frae his theeked biggin takes his way,
Unto the wattl'd fold; whence, to the hill
He drives his fleecy care, to tafte the fweets
O' the bedewed morn.—Now on the hills
The fcorching king of day, his beard difplays
Refulgent, wi' the *birflin* beams o' light.
The fogs affrighted at his burning face,
For refuge, feek the undulating air.
The clouds, light moving o'er the mountain's brow,

Are

Are leſſen'd by his pow'r—and, through' the world,
His boundleſs view ſmites a' wi' fluid gold.
The ra'en, hoarſe-cawing frae the rocky ſteep,
Mounts to the midway air, wi' active wing—
His croaking ſpeaks fair weather—an' invites
The huſbandman to tread the dewy field.
Bent on their toil, the mowers frae their cots
Stump, luſtily—an' o'er the fluſhing mead
Wide ſpreading, ſtretch the long keen-biting ſcythe,
Wi' *ſtrake* an' *ſtane*, ilk treads the yellow vale,
Unto his daily toil.—Upo' the plain,
Low nodding wi' luxuriant herbage, they,
Well arranged ſtan', ſyne, at a ſignal,
Stoop, eager to the taſk, an', now, ahint
Them fling the treaſure wi' heroic ſweep.


Now, up the lifted ſky the potent ſun
Diſſolves to air the cloſe collected miſts,
An,' ſteaming clouds that floated on the hills—
Till through the far ſtretch'd world the bonny day
          Spreads

Spreads forth intenſe.—Who can in ſilence paſs
The viſible return of Heaven's eſteem!—
The gurgling rill, leſs murm'ring, o'er its bed
Runs lauguid.—To the deep the fiſh repair,
To ſhield them frae the heat o' the riſing day;
An', to the ſlimy pool the paddocks hap
Wi' haſt'ning might, where, underneath the brow
They, ſilently, defy the ardent noon.—
Frae the low, wat'ry, vale, thy eyes direct
Unto the diſtant hills.—Wide o'er the *fells*,
The flocks relaxed by the heat of day,
Lay down their languid ſides.—Some to the heath
Scud nimbly, where, underneath the ſhade
O' buſhy heather they, concealed, ly,
Till cooler hours ariſe.—Some on the brow
O' the ſteep, ſhady, rock, recumbent, paſs
The ſultry hours—an' ſome ahint a craig
Stan' ſnugly, ſhaded frae the burning day;
An' rub their yeuky rumples on the turf.—
Meanwhile the ſhepherd, on the foggy knowe

His

## SUMMER.

His weary limbs reclines, in drowſy mood.
His faithfu' dog, hard by, amuſive, ſtalks
The benty brae, ſlow, liſt'ning to the chirp
O' wand'ring mouſe, or moudy's carkin hoke.
Now, to the ſhade, the feather'd tribe repair,
Wi' feeble wing.—Upo' the aged oak,
The crow ſpreads out his feathers to the ſun—
While, hid among its leaves, the gouk ſits mute,
Wi's *wiſe-horn* dry, waiting the caller tide,
Wherein, to pleaſe his mate by's auld, *cuckoo*.

Thus far, bra Muſe! thou'ſt ſung—but don't diſdain
To let the little, feeble, ſummer-race,
Share in thy ſong, and, flutter in thy lay.
Mov'd by the potent heat the infect tribe
Fly frae their ſecret caves, wi' pow'rfu' wing—
Frae every darkſome chink wherein they ſlept,
The wint'ry hours away, the reptiles creep
In myriads, baſking in the ſunny ray.
Far frae his wattled home, th' carefu' bee
Strays to the flow'ry dale, to cull the wealth

## SUMMER.

O' the fair spreading broom—the beaming day
Invites to industry.—Frae bloom to bloom
The industrious insect plys his little wings;
While, up the *howes* the bummles fly in troops,
Sipping wi' sluggish trunks, the coarser sweets,
Frae rankly-growing bri'ers an' bluidy-fingers.
Great is the humming din—but, should a cloud
Rise in the wat'ry south, an' o'er the field
Emit its pearly pow'r, the busy world
Forsake their honied tasks, an', homeward skim
The wide extended plain.—Quick to his house
Each hastens, to avoid the wat'ry death—
An' 'tween their portals, wi' *theatric press,*
The humming multitude, fast, urging, crowd;
The clouds dispers'd—again the yellow day
Shines forth wi' greater force.—The infant tribe
Maturely wing'd, tir'd wi' their nursery,
Long to possess a kingdom of their own—
Hence, frae the crowded skep they wing their way,
A' bizzing, joyfully, at freedom gain'd.
                                        Adown

Adown a glen, clofe by a wood,
An honeft wabfter's cottage ftood,
Whafe haffet, a Kilmarnock hood
    Kept warm an' fnug;
Sic as his *fore-bears* fin' the flood,
    Clapt o'er their lugs.

Right bien John liv'd in his poffeffion—
Nae brither weaver o' profeffion,
Wad mair than he fcorn, a tranfgreffion
    By night or day—
Than he nane e'er in, the Kirk-Seffion,
    Had mair to fay.

Like ither honeft godly folk,
John wad hae laugh'd, and, told his joke,
An', wi' his neighbour ta'en a *fmoke*,
    Or, gien a fang.
He'd rant till he was like to choke,
    At, " *Jenny dang.*"
        His

His tenement it was but fma'—
Aught fcrimpit roods, an' that was a'—
An' yet his wife was always bra',
     An', unco noof,—
His weans nae duddy figns did fhaw,
     Nor, poortith proof.


Contented wi' his ain kail yeard,
For greater wealth ne'er fafh'd his beard,
His wife did tent the barley breard,
     His bairns the bees,
While he, the plaiddin knotty fheard,
     Juft at his eafe.


While *luckies* at the hallan tapt
Wi' routh o' wark, John heez'd his cap,
An', gied the claith the ither chap,
     Till, fpool an' wheel
O'er Poverty cam, fic a whap,
     As, made him reel.

John was right mod'rate in his notions;
(An upright heart is true devotion)
An', did defpife the outward lotion
     Of haly water,
As nae mair fit for renovation,
     Than, fowin fplatter.


True to his Kirk, he called fools
A' innovators on her rules—
At *Mountaineers* that preach on ftools,
     He coudna wink—
Quoth John " They ply their wily tools
     But for the *chink*."


The Sun had reach'd his mid-day tow'r,
Clouds black an' heavy 'gan to low'r—
John, nothing dreading frae the pow'r
     Of the noon-day,
Unto the Kirk had, at the hour,
     Gaen forth to pray.
       The

# SUMMER.

The good man's prayers are often mar'd
Though frae the warld his thoughts be barr'd—
An', true devotion oft is fcar'd
     By beaft or boggle;
An' th' heart which has wi' vice juft war'd,
     Is fet a goggle.


The clouds difperfing 'fore the *fin*,
Wha hetly o'er the *lift* did rin,
The bees wi' awfu' *cafting* din,
     Rofe wi' a wheel,
An', in a han-clap crofs'd the lin
     Straught aff to fcreel.


Faft to the Kirk the callan birl'd,
An,' the door fnack he quickly twirl'd,
Syne, at his dady loudly fkirl'd,
     " They're out o' fight!"
Mefs John's twa lugs right fairly dirl'd,
     Stunn'd wi' the fright.

John naething faid, but took his bonnet—
As *needfu' work* he look'd upon it—
Let ither people tauk an' drone it,
      E'en as they pleafe—
'Twas what few i' the Kirk wad fhunned
      Were their the bees.


By this his neebor on the lay,
Tam Cleg, his wife, and, twa three mae,
Were got upo' the hawthorn brae
      Wi' key an' *girdle*,
An', a white claith weel ftuff'd wi' ftrae,
      Upo' a hurdle.


Some this way ran acrofs the dell,
An' that way others fcour'd the *fell*—
John ften'd the burnie by himfel,
      Wi' eerie brow;
But, of the hive none e'er cou'd tell,
      Or where, or how.

       'Tis

'Tis ardent noon, an' now, throughout the plain
The languid husbandmen, oppress'd wi' heat,
Lean faintly o'er their toil—The mowers, now,
Half o'er the *cutting* task, supinely ly
Upo' the shorn swaird, regardless for
An hour, of pain or care—in hale enjoyment
O' stout feaming *swats* an' plenteous fare.
Among the springing grain the weeders walk
Dowy an' feeble.—Scarce through the leafy brake
Is heard a murmur.—In yon distant glade,
The Sun, refulgent, strikes the pearly stream,
Dazzling to the sight—Through blooming Nature
Bright blazing day pervades—an' pow'rfu', strikes
The spreading blossom wi' his fervent glow.
The weary traveller through sweat an' sun,
Oppress'd, gladly reclining on the hallan-stane,
Sips, cautiously, his mug o' *tippenny*.
Frae towns an' distant villages thick crowds
Press, thronging, to the Fair, to pass the day

## SUMMER.

In harmlefs merriment.—The reaming caups
Are nimbly handed round,—an' focial mirth
Sits, fidging, on ilk turf throughout the hill.

  The rifing Sun upo' the fells [hills struck through]
   Right bonnily was blinkin,
  When Rab an' Jeany by themfels
   Unto the Fair were linkin.—
  Wi' bra white ftockings on his legs,
   Rab fhow'd his knotted garters—
  Sae dainty was his bonny Jean,
   Nae lafs was ever fmarter

       Or blythe, that day.

Alang

Alang the way they walk'd fu' gay,
    An' talk'd their loves thegether;
Rab aft wad fing, but, Jean wad fay,
    " Firſt let us aſk my mither."—
Wi' han' in han' the plain they ſcour'd,
    Like any partraicks pairing,
Unto the *Hill*, whare, crowds did pour,
    A' for to get a fairing
                Unſeen, that day.


An' ſic a fight ſure ne'er was ſeen,
    O' lads an' ruddy laſſes,
Some thither went to ſhow their ſhoon,
    An' ſome to tak their glaſſes.
Upo' the *Hill*, nags, men, an' boys
    A' through ither faſt did bicker—
Some *here* ſat ſelling Tunbridge toys,
    An' *there* ſome ſat wi' licker
                In kaigs, that day.

An', there was ginger-faced Moll,
    Wi *sweeties* frae Kirk\*\*\*bree—
An' Ca'f-reed carrier Samuel Noll,
    Nae better than he should be.—
An', there was nimble-finger'd Ben,
    Wha frae the whins cam jumpin,—
An', beggars frae the auld Brig-en',
    Amang the croud cam limpin
                To thieve, that day.


An' there was pluke-fac'd Willie Kell,
    Wi' brandy in a barrel,—
An' Jemmy Neal an' Geordy Fell,
    Wha baith cam there to quarrel—
An' there fat leering Lilly Scot
    Upo' a green truff laughin—
Wha sold at tippence-plack the pot
    The best yill i' the clachan,
                Sae brisk, that day.

Great

## SUMMER.

Great was the noife of chapman lads—
    An,' muckle was the buffle;
Wi' girls wi' gingerbread in dauds,
    An' boys wi' baubee whuffles.—
Some tippling chiels gaed to the tent,
    To hanfel Leezy Waldron;
An', drank until their wymes were ftent,
    Like any drum or cauldron,
            Wi' punch, that day.


The laffes, now, in twas an' threes,
    Cam fweating up the entry;
Nell, Jean, an' Sue, frae Ba\*\*\*ghie
    An' fic *mifca'ed* gentry.—
Their fweethearts met them at the gate;
    Juft at the hour expected—
But fquintin Sufy took the pet,
    Becaufe, fhe was neglected,
            An' fcorn'd that day.

                Ned

## SUMMER.

Ned Toozy frae the " Cock an' Breeks,"
    A noble tent erected,—
He screw'd his tongue within his cheeks,
    An' said he much expected—
Ned's sign upo' the riggin *flaff"d*,
    While he within was chearin,—
The lasses 'tween their fingers laugh'd,
    An' said it was a queer ane,
              An' strange, that day.


Wi' feaming swats upo' a sod,
    Sat highland Andrew Tamson,
An' in a quarry by the road,
    Sat winsome Willie Samson.
Willie was a racklefs chiel,
    An' that the neebors ken'd ay,—
An,' be the tweelie what it will,
    Bra Willie wad defend ay
              Himsel, that day.

                Upo'

# SUMMER.

Upo' the hill-tap by himsel
    Tam Tapster fix'd his staning—
Sic was the pow'r o' Tapster's yill,
    It set ilk heart a langing.—
Peg Pharis had, to quench her drouth,
    But pri'd it—an' amazing!—
Its vertue spread about her mouth,
    An', set her bluid a blazing
              *Elsewhere,* that day.


Up cam twa spanky countra lairds,
    Upo' their fillies mounted—
Ane might discern by their beards,
    How mony years they'ad counted.
Now up an' down throughout the fair,
    They crack'd their eel-skin lashes;
An' gayly show'd their raploch gear,
    An', bridles made o' rashes,
              Weel twin'd, that day.

                    Now

## SUMMER.

Now, through the crowd cam Jocky Day,
    The laird o' Allanbankie—
Wi's lac'd cravat he look'd right gay;
    In troth his nae fheep-fhankie—
As Jocky paffed through the *flap*,
    Rab Sinkler loud did hollow—
Ilk lafs cock'd up her filken cap,
    Saying, daikins! here's the fellow
            For *them*, that day.


Young Andrew Mar o' Brechan-howe
    Cam there to fell his filly,
An' having little in his pow,
    Took up wi' racer Nelly—
Poor Andrew ta'en wi' Nelly's charms,
    Coft her gillore of raifins,
But, Nelly fled frae 'tween his arms,
    An' aff wi' Gib the Mafon
            Flegg'd faft, that day.

# SUMMER

Up cam Tam Tell an' Sutor Sam,
    High cap'ring, frae the vennal,
As tent upo' the *aftergame*,
    As, hounds loos'd frae a kennel—
Sam, glowrin, ftumped through the thrang
    To meet his lafs Meg Michan,—
Her prefence gi'd his heart a bang,
    An', fet it a' a pechan
            Wi' joy that day.


The laird of Crae, an' twa three drones,
    Cam fliding through the dockens,
An', lap the dyke, ftraught up to S\*\*\*n's
    Their morning drouth to flocken—
The laird, a fheep's-e'e cooft on Jean,
    Auld mantin Michael's daughter,
His heart to kifs her fair did *green*,
    Yet, coudna fpeer wha aught her,
            Sae blate, that day.

                      But

## SUMMER.

But now the glomin coming on,
    The chiels began to pingle,—
An' drunken carls coupin down,
    Made mugs an yill-caups jingle—
The Widow Broddy by the flap,
    Wha fold the tartan preen-cods,
By Whifky mauld, lay *but* her cap,
    Her head upon a green fod,
                Right fick, that day.


A hurly burly now began,
    An' cudgels loud were thumpin—
The gazing crowd together ran
    O'er cranes o' nackets jumpin—
Then cam a batch o' wabfter lads
    Frae " Rodney's Head" careerin,
Wha gied them mony a donfy blaad
    Without the caufes fpeerin
                O' the fray, that day.

# SUMMER.

Up Watty-Bodkin wi' a rung,
   Cam like a lion rampin—
An' 'tween his teeth his flav'rin tongue
   Fu' faft he kept a champin—
Now Watty, tho' a taylor bred,
   Was ane o' rackless mettle—
He lap the *ftans* to Willie Gled
   An' foon the tweelie fettl'd
             *But* bluid that day.

## SUMMER.

Such was the iſſue of the jovial day.
Now ſwarm the ruſtics o'er the bluſhing vale,
Intent to reap the bounty, o' the mead.—
Now, hand in hand, in ſocial chat, walk forth,
Both men an' maidens, youthfu', to the toil.—
Behind the mowers, ſome, wi' carefu' hands
Diſperſe the ſwairded herbage to the ſun.
Hence, through the breathing harveſt, row on row,
Appears the tedded grain.—Unto the day
Some ſpread the humid locks—while ſome wi' rakes,
The balmy ruſſet hay, mellow an' ſweet,
Thick o'er the ſhorn plain in cocks collect.
Sic bliſsfu' ſcenes of labor and of love,
Of ſocial glee and merriment, the ſons of health,
In their retirement, happily enjoy.—
Such ſcenes of rural mirth, and rural peace,
Are much unken'd to the voluptuous cit,
Whoſe pleaſure is confin'd within the walls
Of, throng commercial life—whoſe only joy
Is hoarded in his ſcrip aboon his gold.

Now

# SUMMER.

Now to the hills the ruddy band break forth,
Joyfu' an' ſtrong, an' in the wattled fold
The harmleſs flocks convene.—Frae hill to hill
The bleating din is heard, doleful an' wae—
Lambs for their mothers mourning, an' the yowes
Dreading a ſeparation, to the hills
Caſt o'er their ſhou'ders many a wiſhfu' glance,
Frae eyes fu' ſwell'd wi' true maternal love.
Into the *pen* the timid flocks are hurl'd—
An', now, upo' their panting, tawdry, ſides,
The ſhears ply nimbly, wi' inceſſant twang.
Ye harmleſs race! it is for needy *man*
Ye're of your fleeces rob'd—Be not afraid—
'Tis not the ſlaught'rous gully 'bove your heads
That's lifted—'Tis the gently moving hand
Of tender-hearted ſwain, which o'er your ſides
Guides the keen *cowing* ſhears.—When meekly to
  The all-bereaving hand ye've laid your hips,
Ye ſhall again your former freedom find;
An', leave, to wander on your well-known hills.

## SUMMER.

Nature now pants beneath the potent fun—
The parched clod, expofed to the day,
Is of its vegetation nip'd.—The cleaving fields
And wide extended plains gape, wi' the pow'r
O' the all-conq'ring noon.—The purling ftream
Scarce murmurs o'er its pebbles—and, the hills,
Seen thro' the floating blaze, appear to fmoke.
Thrice blefs'd the fwain, who, in the *caller fide*
O' th' tow'ring hill, can ftretch his weary limbs,
Regardlefs o' the heat—or, in the fhade
O' th' leafy foreft can fupinely ly,
An' whiftle every forrowing care awa.
Retire my Mufe! into the middle gloom
Of yonder diftant wood, where grows the oak,
Talleft an' broadeft to the blufhing year,
On whofe fair top, the culver, fitting, coos
His woodlan' notes, expreffive, to his mate.
There, in the awfu' fhade fits folemn Peace.
There is the place where Meditation dwells!
Far frae the *world* retir'd, the honeft foul

## SUMMER.

Sits ruminating on the ways of men;
An' thro' the gloom of thick embow'ring trees,
Aspires the brightness of a world unknown.

Black o'er the sky the rolling clouds pervade;
An', 'fore the sun their sable mantle spread.
Frae pole to pole, the lengthen'd gloom is stretch'd,
Creative of dismay.—Aloud the peals
Of thunder now athwart the *lift* is heard,
Tremendous to the ear—an', cloud on cloud,
Compelled by the rending light'ning's rage,
Rush on, " in furious elemental war."—
Hence wi' conflictive storm, upo' the plains
Down fa' the pearly drops o' nipping hail.
Disolv'd in liquid streams, the torrent swells
High o'er its banks, an' lays the verdant vale
In one continued deluge.—Often on
The wide distended plain, the farmer casts
His woefu' eye, while, down the rolling stream
He views the labors o' his carefu' hands,

Borne on the wave, an' in the ocean loſt.

Frae the gray bank, where willows intertwine
Wi' ſedge an' ruſhes, o'er the limpid pool,
The wild-duck, rouſed by the fowler's tread,
Faſt flaughters, quacking, to the farther ſhore;
While to the lake, her little gorlin brood
*Pieping* diſtreſs, pop headlong in the flood,
An' dive for ſafety.—On the humid bank
The fiſherman purſues his lonely trade;
An' to the flood flings forth his luring bait,
To tempt the *ged*.—Where now the ſwelled tide
Enſkirts the borders o' the buſhy bank,
And in the corners o' the ſhorn mead
Encircles in a pool, there, with the breeze,
Fling forth thy hook, deck'd with the peacock gem.
Should now the hungry chieftain o' the deep
Eſpy the well-deck'd fly, aſkance he views't
Wi' wiſhfu' eye, an' as it ſkims the flood
Around his head, wi' ardent wheel he turns,
An' plunges, eager, on the buſked death.

To

## SUMMER.

To tread the verdant bank in summer-heat—
Wi' pliant rod to lash the crystal flood;
An', drag the finny captives to the shore—
Is exercise right fondly to be wish'd.


As frae the face of the obscured heaven
The scatter'd clouds disperse, the azure sky
Appears, expressive, of a bonny day.
All Nature, cheared by the bright'ning sun,
Shines forth wi' greater lustre, calm an' pure,
Diffusing through the universe her gifts—
An', o'er the fields in yellow robes of joy,
Displays the beauties o' the plenteous year—
'Tis glorious all, an' beautifu' around—
Through verdant vales the pleasing sound is heard,
Of lowing herds—while bleating flocks, upo'
The hills, thick spreading, join the gratefu' song
To charm the list'ning ear—An' shall not man,
Whose joys are more exalted, an' whose bliss
Is of a purer *cast*—who o'er the world

Perceives the tempest ceas'd, an' peace restor'd,—
Shall he, unthankfu', sit, an' unconcern'd,
Neglect to chant the wonders of that *hand*,
Which, chang'd the storm into an azure calm;
And, hush'd the thunder into milder day!
The sun, now downward on the western main
Lets fall his yellow rays, shot, mildly, o'er
The distant hills, wi' animating warmth—
The fleeting clouds, in beauteous robes bedeck'd,
Incessant roll athwart the sky serene—
While o'er the verdant fields, the idle *world*
Slow moving walk, to taste the vital breeze;
An' pass, in social chat, the ev'ning-hour—
Some, now, upo' the mountains, lonely, love
To walk, an' meditate on Nature's Works—
There in the rugged wilderness, where, in
The mountain daisy, or the creeping bri'r,
They may behold, to harmonize the heart;
An' raise their gratefu' praises up to heav'n.
Some o'er the fertile valley chuse to walk

Amidst

Amidſt the richer fragrance—while, ſome love
Upo' the river's winding bank to ſtray;
An', breathe their meditations o'er the ſtream.
At this cool hour of day, the *village* ſwarms
Exulting, on the green,—ilk on his play
An' fav'rite pleaſure bent.—Some *han'* to *nieve*,
Wi' manly pith o' arm, beyond the mark,
Far fling the pond'rous *mell*.—Leſs valid, ſome,
Though not leſs dext'rous, on the *padder'd* green,
Frae *doon* to *doon*, ſhoot forth the penny-ſtane.
Thus, on his ſport intent, each honeſt heart
Exulting, bids the gladſome ſtreams of joy,
An', ſocial mirth, diffuſe upo' the plain.
Unto the ſhaded grove the nymphs an' ſwains
Wi' a' the rural train in troops repair,
To play at *buff*.—The ſhaded, cool, retreat,
Invites to ſocial ſport.—The mirthfu' choir
Around the *hood-wink'd* ſwain a' hooting run,
Ilk ſtriving to eſcape his wily catch.—

Ane plucks his sleeve, another, dauntlefs, stands
Within an arm's-length o's blin'-folded face—
His fav'rite nymph, wi' glad, uplifted, heart,
Stands *chirtin*, in a corner, longing much
To feel his lov'd embrace—Quick sighted he
In love, led by the laugh, fast to his breast
Enclasps the willing maid.—Thus pafs the hours
In joyous play, an' leal familiarity.

" Right winsome was the simmer e'en'
  " When lads and lasses pingle
" An' coupin carls on the green
  " An' dancing round the ingle—
" The laird o' Mumfield merry grew,
  " An' Maggy Blythe was fainer—
" An' Michael wi' a mather fu'
  " Crys " Welcome to the manor."


" They whisk'd about the good brown ale,
  " An' bumper'd round the claret—
" The whisky ran frae reaming pails—
  " Some lasses got their skair o't—
" The cook-maid she was wond'rous spruce,
  " An' bobbed in the entry—
" She wadna taste it *butt* the house,
  " But pried it in the pantry.

An'

" An' now, the glomin comin on
   " The lasses turned skiegh, man,—
" They hid themsels amang the corn,
   " To keep the lads abeigh, man—
" But Maggy, wha fu' well did ken,
   " The lurking Latherins' meaning,
" Put a' the lads upo' the scent,
   " An' bade them stanch their *greening*.


" Weel kilted frae a breckan bufs
   " Up started Rosy Dougan,
" As tent as, if she had been a pufs,
   " An' ilk yaul chiel a grewhun—
" So ho! they cry'd—away they went,
   " She led them sic a string, man—
" Syne turn'd about, an' hameward sten'd,
   " A' pechan in a ring man.

Sue

" Sue Cumberlaw an' Helen Don
    " In jumping o'er a dyke, man,—
" Fell, belly-flaught, on Doctor John
    " Wha cur'd the rumple-fyke, man—
" Poor Helen she fell in a trance—
    " The Doctor twice did stumble,—
" He skilfully pu'd out his lance
    " An' cur'd her o' the tumble.


" Upon a truff sat Leezy Card,—
    " The Landlord he sat nieft her,—
" He on her sleely stroak'd his beard,
    " While mantin Michael mist her—
" O doughty Landlord ! Ilay cries,
    " My titta ye will ruin—
" Ne'er fash your beard, the dame replies—
    " There is no harm a doing."

The

## SUMMER.

The fun has loft his pow'r, and now, apace
Sinks 'yond the weftern hills.—The fhade of night
O'erfpreads the wide domain.—The lowing herds
Unto the *loans* repair—And, in the brake
The feather'd tribes pop, quietly, to reft.
Now filence o'er the world prevails.—And, now,
All Nature foaks refrefhment from the dew
O' the cool, nightly hours.—Man to his home
Wi' weary limbs repairs—and, in his cot
Reclining, till the dawn, in eafefu' fleep,
Contented, hails the day;—and, joyfully,
Renews the labor of his humble lot.

## AUTUMN.

# AUTUMN.

FAIR to the sight, across the yellow plain,
  Rich Autumn comes in, bounty-bearing dress.
Rank-spreading Summer's vegetative green,
Now ripens into dusky plenteousness.
Led on to gratefu' praise, my reed I tune,
Wi' merry heart.—Whate'er the mellowing frost,
In Winter's cold, purgative, had prepar'd,
And Summer's sun had caus'd to blossom forth,
Low-bending now, luxuriant to the view,
Excites my rustic Muse, and swells her song.

When equal are the hours of night and day,
And, *Ceres* balances the circling year,
Departed Summer, o'er the lifted sky,
Leaves a serener hue.—Sweet beams arise,
Of lucid, pleasing light—while, o'er the glebe,

## AUTUMN.

By kind attemp'ring *funs*, the ripen'd corn
Spreads forth its ears, extenfive. Richly they
Stand in the early dawn—and, to the eye
Afford a plenteous fight—exciting praife.


'Tis morn—filent and thick the bending ftore
Leans o'er the yellow field—and, not a ftalk
Is feen to wag, fave, by the bunting-lark,
Or hungry fparrow. To the golden light,
Th' bounteous harveft lends the heavy head;
And, dew-drop'd fields wide glitter with the day.
" A calm of plenty! till the ruffled air
" Falls from its poife, and, lets the zephyrs blow"
The fanning weft-wind rends the darken'd *lift*;
And, dufky clouds, along the fky obfcur'd,
Fly fcatter'd.—To the foftly-fweeping breeze,
The fleecy mantle yields, born gently on,
Like downy flakes, athwart the thiftly field.
The day advancing, fhines upo' the plain;
And, gilds the flufhing harveft.—To the eye,

## AUTUMN.

As far as the extended prospect shoots,
The waving warld displays its chequer'd face;
Rolling luxurious in a flood of grain.


Red frae the east the sun begins to peep—
The reapers, drowsy, and, wi' ropy eyes,
Start frae their thatched cots, and, to the bent
Swarm forth, accoutred for the lab'rous toil.
The *horn* is out—loud *blasts* the valleys fill;
And, *morning calls* spread through each neighb'ring
    field.
The master's voice bestirs the lazy lass,
With rankled thumb, and, weary *worked* wrist;
And, at a word, all hands in toil unite.
" This morning bodes us ill," an auld wife cries—
" For see! the sun is *setting* ere he *rise*."
" 'Tis true forsooth," another straightways says—
" For, the gray crow flew o'er our midden tap,
" An,' croak'd his hollow notes before the ra'en."
" But hear ye me," crys *lucky*, on the *heel*—
                        " The

" The ſtars yeſtreen, ſhot weſtlin down the lift;
" And, fell like *fumert's ſpuing*, on the bog."—
'Tis a' o'er true—their bodings, and, their ſpells,
Raiſe up the De'il, and hence, the wind and ſtorm.
Black frae the South, a hurricane is ſeen
To ſweep the heathy fells, and, ſcroggy braes—
Its face fraught with deſtruction.—Through the *band*
'Tis wild concern, and, dire amazement all.
The ſcene is chang'd—each flings his ſickle by.
Some bind up ſheaves, and ſome in heaps them caſt—
One forms the *ſtook* wi' nice-directing eye,
Another following after, crowns with *hoods*—
Thus, through the field, in a tumult'ous throng,
Their pliant hands, work nimbly out their taſk.
Now labor's huſh'd.—The pearly drops fa' thick;
An', ſurly blaſts invigorate their force.
To 'ſcape the ſtorm, ſome to the hedge repair—
Others unto the *ſtooks* for ſhelter, flee.
Ane ſcours the plain, well kilted to the *baw*,

Striving,

# AUTUMN.

Striving, wi' hafty ftrides t'outrun the ftorm—
While others, in defiance of the day,
Chuckle together, underneath the ftraw.
Fafter and fafter falls the pearly ftorm;
And, fhuts the mafter's hopes in clouds of rain.
A fruitlefs day! Now, hameward all return,
Wi' each his fickle on his collar fix'd;
And, round the warm hearth, in hafte repair—
A dripping crowd.—Some parched fuel bring—.
One flings on turf—another ftirs the coals.
All now are wet, and, all would fain be dry—
Meanwhile, the cau'dron-pot, brimful of *roots*,
Is from the ingle ta'en, and ftraight again,
The active part commences.—Thud on thud,
The fonorous *beetle* on the metal clangs;
And, champs, deftructive.—Now the fignal giv'n,
Each plays his part, wi' fhining morning face;
And great's the noife of boys, and fpoons, and dogs.
Wi' paunch well ftuff'd, all penfive care's forgot;
And, " *fwaggering, roaring Willy*" crowns the day.

# AUTUMN.

Far in the corner of a shelt'ring wood,
Remote frae care, the young Maria, on
Whose face, the bloom of beauty spread, did with
Her aged Mother dwell.—Maria's charms
Shone like the radiance o' a summer's morn'
Upo' the balmy rose.—Unspotted *worth*,
And, modest *virtue*, on her lovely brow
Sat gracefu'—Frae the power o' selfish pride,
An', giddy passion, free—content, she past
The joyfu' minutes of, her blushing years.
Upon her mother, *eild*, and *poortith* had,
Usurp'd their rudest sway.—In solitude
They liv'd, retir'd, amidst surrounding shades,
Unthought of, as unseen, save by the heart
Of Colin, wha, amang the neighb'ring hills,
Did tend, a wee wheen sheep.—The honest swain,
Whose heart was innocent, no passions knew.
Who nought of Fortune could with others brag,
Save, health and sweet content—wad often gang
Among the spreading broom, and, to the winds
Effuse his plaintive tale.—Maria's charms

The

# AUTUMN.

The live-lang-day he'd fing—and, when at eve',
Driving his wethers to the wattled fold;
Stumping along, he'd whiffle what he fang.'
Oft' as, among the bufhy birny braes,
Young Colin plodded wi', his ftrayed tips,
He'd caft a look upo' the lonely cot,
Wi' wifhfu' een—and, in pretended hafte,
Wad *tap* the hallan wi' his hazle kent;
And, fpeer gin they had feen his bawfant ram.
Refpect long fhown, had ripen'd into love—
Maria's heart was Colin's—Colin's her's—
And, nor the fmiles nor frowns of Fortune, could
Disjoin the juft alliance.—Who can count
The number of their charms—or, who can tell
The greatnefs of their blifs, whom love unites?
Maria's virtue fhone in, ilka deed;
And, Colin fang her beauty, on his reed.
The happy twa, fae blifsfu', fae content,
Had ta'en each other's oath, ay to prove true.—
Entwin'd in love, Maria had nae fear.—
Beneath the fpreading boortree's cooling fhade,

# AUTUMN.

She turn'd her spinning-wheel, while, Colin, on
The foggy fells, pursu'd his *fleecy care*.
Ay heartsome baith, they pass'd the day, in hope,
To close the e'ening in, each other's arms.
But who can tell the scenes o' good or ill,
That, may befa' the best?—The ways of Heav'n
Are intricate, e'en to a *shepherd's* tread;
And Providence oft gets into *one* scale,
To keep the proper poise, when, easfu' bliss,
Into the *other*, sosses, overpond'rous.


Five Moons (it was nae mair) had scarce renew'd,
Their weather-blunted horns, till Colin felt,
His treasure lessen, and, his cares increase.
His little crop, the spate had borne away—
His cattle died—his sheep their hills forsook;
And, roaming wildly wide, mix'd with the flocks
Of distant fremmit folds.—By need compell'd,
(For sheer Necessity's commands are strong)
Colin and Maria their cottage left;

      And,

## AUTUMN.

And, both wi' looks direct on *better* days,
Went forth to labor, in Glenalvon's fields.
The pride of Dee, and, of the neighb'ring swains,
Glenalvon was—the friendly, and, the good—
Whose heart, frae selfish passion, ay was free;
And, relish'd rural life in a' its joy.
As here and there, pleas'd wi' his yellow riggs,
The swain behind his jovial *band* did walk;
Praising the *snoddest cut* frae *point* to *heel*—
The fair Maria drew his love-struck eye—
He saw, and lov'd her—but, nor could his heart,
Nor philosophic confidence avow,
The chaste desire, which, in his bosom rose.
He view'd her, lovely, and, he strove to hide
The sparklings o' his passion—but, the more
He tri'd to smother what her charms had fir'd,
The more it rose in, an all-spreading blaze.
With downcast modesty, Maria turn'd
Her face, frae the glad gazings o' the swain;
Who, walk'd unconscious of a rival pow'r;

And, look'd, and lov'd, the lang autumnal day.
Colin, who never dream'd of jealoufy,
Wi' unfufpecting heart, and, pliant hands,
Clofe by his fair Maria work'd an' fang;
Who, now forgetting trouble in their joy,
Did chafe in mirth, the tedious hours away.
Glenalvon's heart being with the beauteous *fair*,
His paffion's pow'r no longer could conceal—
Hence, in a firm defiance o' the fcorn,
And, the dread laugh the world and felfifh life,
Might fcatter on his choice—thus, mufing, faid—
" What muckle pity! fic a lovely form,
By beauty model'd, and, by virtuous fenfe
Enliven d, 'bove the vulgar of thy fex,
Should be the partner of fome ruftic clown;
And, to a lab'rous tafk, in fweat and fun,
Expos'd, for which, thy hands were never meet.
For thee, fweet maid! I could my lot demean,
To fhare the office of the broiling day—
For thee, lay down my every claim to wealth;

And,

And, count thy *love* alone, a dowry good.
For thee, for thou'rt the pride of goodnefs' felf,
I could, unmurm'ring, live—with pleafure die."
Thus did the fwain ejaculate—and, ftill
On's raxed heart Maria's lovely charms,
And, fair bewitching form, impulfive, came.
But who can paint the lover, when he found
By ftrict enquiry, from herfelf, that fhe
Had pledg'd her troth, her love, her all, to Colin.
A cruel fearch! Sad on his love-fwell'd foul
Was the intelligence.—" Who can declare
The mingled paffions that furpriz'd his heart,
And, through his nerves in fhiv'ring tranfport ran?"
Then wild defpair took place of foothing hope;
And, fad defponding fear o'erfpread, his love.
Yet now, ev'n now, he ey'd the beauteous maid,
Wi' a' the fortitude a generous foul,
Befet with difappointment, could exert—
And, as he view'd her, wifhfu', to his fight,
Her blufhing beauty rofe in, higher bloom.

## AUTUMN.

A fruitlefs glare! Glenalvon's heart which, knew
Not aught that was untrue, with goodnefs fraught,
Kind, rapturous, and juft, to Colin pour'd
The friendly, fair, effufions of his foul.

" Thrice happy fwain—blefs'd with thy nymph fo
  fair—
If *envy* be not *criminal,* I envy *thee.*
Long may your loves harmonioufly entwine,
Around the palm of peace.—Like ivy, may
Your ev'ry leal intent, ay upwards creep,
Along the branches of ftill-blooming truth;
A pleafing evergreen in winter's cold,
When, fruit and leaves fall off difhonefty.
Too long remote from my attention, have
Maria's charms been hid.—Too long, indeed,
Within the covert of yon cot, obfcure,
Has that fair image of much honeft worth,
Liv'd on penurious fare!—But, let me, now,
Frae the fequefter'd wild, and, winter-fide
Of a bleak defert, lead the living fprout,
          Into

# AUTUMN.

Into a richer foil.—Thefe fields which ye
Now labor in, in fervile ftate, are mine.
The flocks of yonder mountains, which, you fee
Among the walys browfing, all are mine—
A bount'ous favour of all-gracious Heav'n.
Though poverty's cold blaft, and, biting ftorm,
Have nip'd the beauty of, your budding charms—
Tranfplanted fafe into a warmer clime,
The bloom fhall fhoot again—and, happinefs,
By renovating *funs* refume her feat.
Then, fling the fickle by, from that fair hand,
But ill befitted for fuch rugged toil.
Here acres fifty, henceforth, fhall be yours;
And, all within *that fold*—take that yours is;
And, ne'er by recompence, nor favor, think
Ye to requite the gift.—As Heav'n on me
Has lavifh'd much its bounty, fo, fhould I
Exert the pow'r of doing others good.
The hungry rook upon my corn preys—
Among my flocks the ra'en, his maw does fill—

A' on ilk ither truft—and, a' are fed—
Heav'n's bleffings are beftow'd to blefs withal."


The ftorm is o'er.—No more the ftream is feen
To fwell, above its banks.—No more the fields
Around, " lie funk, and flatted in the wave."
No more the deluge deepens, nor, the falls
Of deep-defcending waters, from the hills,
Shall dales, an' valleys terrify, afar,
Wi' the tumultuous roar.—The fhepherd, now,
Unto their native hills collects, his flocks,
Wide fcatter'd by the floods.—The hufbandman
Stalks o'er his fields, all defolate, forlorn;
And, views, relenting, the dire havock, which
Bleak winds and waves have of his treafure made—
And, the poor cottager, by whofe rough hand,
Thefe treafures were collected, mindful of,
The pinching winter unprovided for,
Views, fad, his wheaten labors fcatter'd round;
Or, by involving currents, fwept away.

# AUTUMN.

Now, on the founding warld, the morning fun,
His radiant pow'r diffufes.—With the day,
The fportfman traverfes the heathy hill,
Fu' bent on flaughter.—Here his faithfu' dog
Scours nimbly o'er the plain, and, warily,
With open noftrils, fnuffs the *chuckling* brood.
Wi' earneft look upo' the covey caft,
Firm to his poft, he well-inftructed, ftands,
And, waits the fignal.—Lift'ning in the breeze,
His mafter's tread, the wifh'd for fign' he hears;
And, forth, amain, upo' the latent prey
He, gladly, fprings.—The thund'ring gun up to
The eye is lifted, eagerly, and, as
The circling covey mounts on birring wings,
The filent furges of the liquid air,
Anon, the clam'rous *charge* emits its force;
And, from its tow'ring ftation brings the bird,
A fpreckled treafure, plump, upo' the plain.

While fome delight to brufh the heathy fells
At early dawn, among the churring *pouts*,
                                        Some

## AUTUMN.

Some, lefs inclining the rude hills to tread,
Chufe, rather, through the ftubble rough an' rank,
Around their habitations, to furprize,
The couring partridge.—O'er the timid hare,
Poor, harmlefs beaft! without or caufe, or need,
Some love to fhow their triumph.—Frae the corn,
Beftir'd by clang of fickles, to the *bent*
Scar'd maukin trots, and, now to fome lone haunt
Scuds, trembling, faft.—The way fhe takes is
    mark'd;
And, frae their kennel, the mad, rav'ning pack,
Are, *gowling*, led.—The thick, impearled dew,
Betrays her cunning tread—and, fad and ftrong,
In echoing yelpins, far behind, fhe hears
The onward haft'ning death.—In vain fhe tries,
By frequent mazes, to elude the ftorm,
Th' unfriendly breeze reports.—Down frae the hill,
Unto the wat'ry flats, fhe nimbly fcours—
Wi' weary labyrinths among the fens,
And, many turnings tir'd—afraid to ftop,

                                                She

She to the whins repairs, where, 'mong the broad
An' thick entangling bushes, to the sun
She heaves her sweaty sides.—The fanning gale
Brings the dread sound of sad destruction on.
Nearer and nearer still, is heard the voice
Of horns, and murd'ring hounds.—Now frae the thick
Embow'ring broom, and rank bespreading heath,
She slips, unseen—and o'er the dusky ground,
Wi' wither'd breckans strewed, stens, weary.
Across the thistly plain she takes her way—
Still doubling on her steps, and list'ning, stops,
And, stopping, listens to the coming sound;
And, list'ning, stens again.—Her best effort
Is vain.—The eager pack full-opening, load
The air wi' exclamations—and, the crowd
Exulting to the death, press on with speed,
By toot of horn conducted.—Close upon
The hirpling victim, the loud neighing steed,
Prances, triumphant—and, the hunter's voice,

# AUTUMN.

Tumultuous rais'd, with lash of whips according,
Loud frae the hills the skraiching death resounds.
'Tis savage pleasure this.—But, let not in
The deadly trap, the harmless creature pine;
Nor, in the well-known seat, where, flat, conceal'd,
Wi' wide unsleeping een, secure, she lies,
Deprive her o' her life—'tis Nature's right,
Which life *confers*, as much as man's to *take* it.

WILLY

# WILLY CLEG's ELEGY.

---

OF armour, and the man I fing—
His *gun* well charg'd the truth will ring—
Who beft of a' could downward bring,
>    The birring cock.
Who could whip up, as wi' a ftring,
>    The diving duck.


Bengairn may mourn, and weep, and grane,
The day that Willy 'neath the ftane
Was laid, out-ftreeked, fkin and bane,
>    A lifelefs lump—
Nae mair to fee the partraicks rin
>    Nor maukins mump.

## AUTUMN.

Laſt time I ſaw him on the *bent*,
A maukin roſe before his kent—
He cock'd his piece—the *charge* was lent
     Frae th' horn o' *time*—
But, ah! his *powder* was a' *ſpent*,
     He coudna *prime*.


When ſportſmen on the hills were thrang,
Unto his breeks like drift he'd bang;
And, crave their pardon that, fae lang
     He'd been a fitting—
Syne, ſtraught unto the bent he'd gang,
     To find *her* fitting.


After ilk ſhot he'd tak a drap,
An', bann wi' birr the geezen'd cap,
That, in his wyme left fic a flap
     For want o' licker—
Then, aff the ither cann he'd tap,
     To mak him ficker.
       How

## AUTUMN.

How firſt he learn'd to ſhoot ye'll hear—
The ſhank-bane o' an auld dead mare,
He frae the houghs an' cutes did tear;
     An' in a ſtock
He firmly fix'd it wi' a *ware,*
     *But* pan or lock.


It was in Winter bleak an' ſnell,
An', wreaths o' ſna' upo' the fell,
When guns did crack, an', piſtols knell,
     Adown the glens,
That, Willy dottart by himſel,
     Among the hens.


His gun o' *bane* cloſe by the hallan,
Place did the wild miſchievous callan—
The blow was ettled at a tall ane,
     A bra *ware* cock—
Then, thud! I trow it was a bawl ane;
     It made him rock.

He wi' a lowan ſtick did ſteal,
Among the burdies i' the biel—
His gun he level'd o'er a creel,
     Upo' his doup,—
Then, pop! poor *Rabin* on his keel,
     Did, over coup.


Frae ſma' to great atchievements, men
Right faſt to riſe, we often ken—
Now Willy frae his ain houſe en'
     A wagtail ſhooter,
Wi' *pointers* on the hills did ſten,
     The prince o' pouters.


O Johnny Burd! poor dowy chiel,
What loſs, what ſorrow doſt thou feel!
Left now, among the braes to ſpeel,
     The live-lang day,—
Without thy Willy's mirth to ſteal,
     The hours away!

       Hear

# AUTUMN.

Hear me ye fells an' every cleugh!
Ye ſtubble fields, an' ſcroggy heughs!
An', echo a' 'tween Dee an' Deugh,
     The waefu' maen!
For Willy that was ance ſae teugh,
     But now is gane.

In thund'ring thuds frae's rifle bore,
Among the hills nae mair he'll roar;
Nor, o'er a bicker cry—gillore!
     His *piece* is muffl'd—
Soon as he ſaw the *ſmoke* was o'er,
     Awa he ſhuffl'd.

His *charge* being driv'n, the rammer *hame*,
Along he trudg'd, in hopes o' game;
But, Death, wha maks e'en ſwallows tame,
     Gied him a pat;
An', now he lies without a name,
     Amaiſt forgot.

## AUTUMN.

Now ducks may quaik an' partricks chur,
An' maukins hirple in ilk fur';
Whilkin their fuds wi' muckle ftur,
    *But* fear or dread—
There is nae man to make demur
    Since Cleg is dead.


Could our fa't tears rin down like Dee,
Out o'er our cheeks, great hills o' Cree,
That a' the warld may hear an' fee
    The dreadfu' fa'!
He was the choice o' company
    That's now awa.


O Willy Cleg! 'tis hard to dree
The weary lack an' lofs o' thee;
Yet, fhall thy *name* for ages be
    Remember'd weel,
While breckans grow, or blooms a tree,
    In fight o' Screel.
      Long

# AUTUMN.

Long has the gouk forsook, the spreading wood—
(Perhaps across the *ocean* ta'en his way)
His *mate* sits dowy 'mong the busky firs,
Stroaking her spreckled breast.—No more till Spring
Renews the fields wi' verdure, and, the trees
Wi' lovely foliage, shall she music hear;
Nor, pleasure find, among these lonesome sprigs.
Behold! afar, the scroggy braes display
The ripen'd nuts, in wild luxuriance—
Ye jovial swains, haste to the hazle brow
Of yonder sunny hill.—Bra virgins a'
Engir'd your claiths about ye, trig an' close,
" Fit for the thicket, an' the tangling shrub,"
And hie awa.—With mirth drown care a wee.
Down in yon glen, aboon the winding brook,
Where fa's the water in, hoarse gurgling streams,
The cluster'd, brown-hool'd treasure, hangs. For you,
Fair nymphs, the woodlands wild retune their song;
An', a' the treasure o' the russet lin,
For you, droops, bount'ous, in the silent shade.

'Twas in the bonny harveſt-moon,
  Right fair an' dry the day,
When, lads an' laſſes frae the toon,
  Fu' bent on ſport an' play,
Did to the hazle bank repair,
  The huſky nits to pu'
Wi' ilk his raploch, ſtowing, gear,
  O' poaks, baith auld an' new,
        Weel ſtrung, that day.


Let's a' ſtart fair, cries Rabin Rae,
  That ilk alike may forder—
But, Tibby ſtenning on her tae,
  Pat a' into diſorder.
Now, to the wood they ſkelp wi' might—
  The laſſes wi' their aprons—
An', ſome wi' wallets, ſome wi' weghts,
  An', ſome wi' hoſhens caprin,
        Right heigh, that day.

Of

Of a' the laſſes o' the thrang,
 Nane was ſae trig as Nelly—
E'en ony roſe her cheeks did bang—
 Her leuks were like a lilly—
Right bonny bonny was her mow—
 Her een were flee an' pauky,
Wi' *her* gley'd Tammy wad gae pu'
 Nits—and wi' *her* wad wauk ay,
  Fu' glad, that day.


Nell ſcorned Tam, an' geck'd her head;
 An', boder'd him wi' mocking,—
Syne, fleely glanc'd on Willy Read,
 Wha, lang'd to fill her *ſtocking*.
Willy was a winſome chiel—
 He ken'd the laſs's mind, ay;
An', when the trees ſhe coudna ſpeel,
 Wi's *click* he came behind ay,
  T' aſſiſt, that day.

## AUTUMN.

Ben Blutter was their leader ſtout—
 Amang the ſpreading trees,
Whenever he his horn did toot,
 It ſet their hearts at eaſe.
Beneath the lofty boughs they walk'd,
 A' ſcatter'd here an' there;
Still anſwering each other's tauk,
 To keep their minds frae fear,
    O' ghaiſts, that day.


Great was the ruſtlin din—an' faſt
 The lads their hoſhens pang'd—
Frae bough to bough they nimbly paſt,
 A merry bruſhing thrang.
Ned Shuter, wi' his crabtree kent,
 Fell'd down for Leezy Drew,
Until her apron was ſae ſtent,
 The ſtrings in *targets*, flew,
    About, that day.

     Steen

# AUTUMN.

Steen Tanner ften'd upo' a ftane,
    To view the woody plain;
An', coupin, let an' awfu' grane;
    Maeft feck thought he was flain.
Ilk ran unto the place, to len'
    The lad, a rifan lift—
He hofted ftoutly at *ae* en',
    At tither en' did rift,
              Right loud, that day.


Wi' that a friend near han' cry'd, hoot!
    Syne, at the chiel faft tugged—
The laffes bawl'd "wae worth yere fnoot!"
    An', frae the ftane him rugged—
Meanwhile, beneath them i' the howe,
    Was heard an eldritch cry,
Of, "*plunner plunner bide ye now!*"
    Then aff they a' did hie,
              Wi' fright, that day.

# AUTUMN.

The lasses cooft their shoon, an' scour'd,
 Through gutters, an' through bogs—
Some got ahint a dyke, an' cour'd;
 An', some amang the scroggs.
The *worrycow* gid sic a yell,
 That rair'd frae dale to doon—
*He* got the spuilie to himsel'
 As *they* fled hame to toon,
     Like drift, that day.

# AUTUMN.

Frae ruſtic mirth, amang the diſtant fields,
Now let us tread, the plenteous path of harveſt.
Rich, balmy, and untainted, round the wa's
O' the low-bending orchard, to the ſun
The roſy apples, ſweet, profuſely hang;
An', the ripe mellow pears, frae loaded boughs,
Fa' in inceſſant ſhow'rs before the breeze.
Kind Nature's liberal, all-bounteous hand,
Is ever planting, ever tempering,
The vegetable warld, that earth an' air,
Wi' a' the elemental compoſition mix'd,
May beſt afford great routh o' fragrant ſtores,
For the proud taſte of, ſtill ungratefu' *man*.
Though rich the proſpect this,—yet rather, let
Us walk the ſummit of the diſtant hills,
Far in the wild uprear'd—an', therefrom, view,
In this glad time, the wide extended plains,
Wi' ſun-beams mild adorn'd, which Autumn ſheds
In equal power, o'er the beauteous day.

Upo'

## AUTUMN.

Upo' the ruffet top o' tow'ring Screel,
To breathe the vital air ferene, an' clear,
O! let me ever ftray.—There, Nature dwell
In the grand drefs of mild fimplicity—
Unchang'd by tide or time—an' every view
Frae the afpiring top, diffufive, fpreads
The chequer'd warld in an unbounded fcene.
On yonder wood-fhagg'd hill, the hazle, fpreads
Its fructifying branches to the day;
An', the rich harveft, in the vale below,
Sends forth its bounteous treafure.—*Here* the flocks
In uncheck'd freedom ftray, frae hill to hill;
An', cull the fav'ry blade amang the birns.
An', *there,* the filent herds wi' pleafure roam;
An', fhare a kingdom, rich with artlefs joys.
Here, on the fight, the troubled ocean fwells
Wi' ftorm an' tempeft ftrong.—The briny waves
Ilk ither chafing frae the utmoft Thule,
In fonorous fucceffion, 'gainft the fhore,
High fhelving to the fkies in awfu' roar,

# AUTUMN.

Their foamy thunder scatter.—In the deep,
Perceiv'd afar, the weather-beaten bark
Rolls, lonely, high encompass'd wi' the tide
Of troubled waters.—On the pebbled shore,
The fishermen, drench'd wi' their wat'ry toil,
Wi' sea-weed clad, unto the noon-day sun,
Spread out their tangled nets.—Rough Industry!
Thou bringest blessings; by thy steady hand.
With *thee* in many lab'rous hardships earn'd,
In sun an' sweaty pain, the streams o' wealth,
An' every sweetner o' soft, social life,
Rin unconceal'd.—Thou source of useful arts!
By thee, the wild, rude, barb'rous spirit's taught,
To rise frae savage cruelty, whereon
It rudely fed, mix'd with the beasts of prey;
An' to employ its weel-bestowed powers,
In deeds far less inhuman.—Rous'd by Thee,
Wi' faculties unfolded, Man aspires
Unto the point, which Nature show'd afar
To be attained through the path of art.

Man

Man now by induſtry is taught, to raiſe
Deep hidden treaſure, frae the earth's dark womb.
How in the ardent furnace to diſſolve,
The lumps o' yellow ore—and, how to form,
By ſtrength o' clam'rous *forge*, the current coin—
By *her* he's taught, to turn the torrent's courſe—
To fell the oak, an' chip the ſtately pine—
To ſow the grain, to ſparkle on his board,
In rich o'erflowing nectar poured out—
To chear th' aſpiring ſoul of decent mirth;
An', raiſe the ſoaring mind to things ſublime.

Chang'd are the looks o' the declining year;
An', frae the fields, collecting harveſt ſweeps
The laſt fair handful.—On ilk ruſtic brow,
Pleaſure diffuſive ſheds a chearfu' glance;
An', now the Maſter's hopes being ſafe at home,
Within his well-theek'd barn—ſtrait i' the thrang
He mixes, an' wi' great good humor joins
The ſportive pleaſures o' the jovial *kirn*.

'Tis

# AUTUMN

'Tis Nature's holy-day! The fields now clear'd
O' a' their bount'ous store, th' extended warld,
At rest a wee, speaks glad maternal joy,
In the provision she has amply made;
An', given gratuitously unto her sons.
Within the ha'-house, now, the strains of joy
Are chanted by ilk heart—an', round the furms
In stoups an' caups brimfu', the reaming yill
Is handed nimbly.—Here, baith auld an' young,
Baith men an' maidens, canty carls an' clowns,
Join in the general joy.—The voice of mirth
Unbounded, echoes frae ilk chimla tap;
An', bauks an' kipples ring, wi' festive glee.
A token, this, of gratitude, unfeign'd—
Which, nor the pillar'd dome, nor ample roof
O' luxury, and rich magnificence,
Wherein the heaving heaps o' glitt'ring wealth
Is highly plac'd, can more sincerely give.
An', weel may sic a seafon, sic a day
Of social mirth beget—since all, whate'er
                                    Exalts

Exalts an' chears the heart, that renders life
Delightful in enjoyment, therefrom hangs.
Induſtry by Autumn is matur'd—
Its fruits are ripen'd with the yellow grain,
That overſpread, an' deck, the ſunny field—
By it, the face o' winter, bare an' bleak,
Is rendered leſs awfu'—and, old *Care*,
Chear'd by the look o' *Plenty*, ſocial, ſits,
Securely ſeated by his fire-ſide;
An', hears the whizzing tempeſt rave along.


Forewarned now of Winter's quick approach,
The ſwallow-tribe, on Autumn's duſky garb,
Caſts the laſt look—acroſs the ſky ſerene,
In many turnings, toſſing wide around,
The floating nation ſports—glad that the day,
Calm an' temp'rate, gives them leave to make
The gen'ral muſter, ere they do retire
Into their wint'ry neſts.—Wi' flutt'ring ſpeed
Unto the tiled roof an' chimney-tap,

# AUTUMN.

The journeying multitude in hafte repair—
There, to the fun's departing rays they fpread
Their little wings, an' *chitter* their farewel.
Hence, to a warmer clime they take their way,
Where, with fic ither kindred birds, they dwell,
Until mild Spring's agreeable return
Invites them back again.—In clufters, fome,
Unwilling to forfake their native fheds,
Beneath the fhelving banks, where, nor the wind
Nor Winter's froft can enter, dormant reft.


The hills an' dales by Autumn's fweeping hand
Look on the fight all defolate and wild—
Bleak an' forlorn the once rich, yellow fields,
Now to the eye appear.—Where, lately grew,
The waving harveft, yielding to the breeze
Its bending head, is now a dreary wafte—
The once well-plenifh'd furrow, now becomes
A channel to the fpate, an' rufhing ftorm.
The cattle now, athwart the wat'ry mead

Range uncontroll'd, promifcuous and wide;
An', o'er the ftibbly plain, the nibbling rooks,
In numbers fpread—a fable multitude—
Tugging the fcatter'd ftalks, and cawing dolorous.
Scenes prognofticating thofe of Winter!
But, fee, more ominous than thefe, the leafy wood
In many colours caft—The fpreading afh,
Aforetime fair, green, an' umbrageous to
The weary head o' the way-faring man,
(A fhelter fafe an' fnug frae fun and ftorm)
Now o'er the country round, embrowning, fhakes
Its wither'd robes.—A crowded foliage o'er
The plain lies thick an' dufky.—With the breeze
Frae the matured twig, the ruftlin leaves
Of ev'ry hue fa' thrang, an' through the warld
The awfu' ruling feafon fhows its pow'r,
In leaf-ftrown walks of lonely devaftation.

Thefe, to a mind contemplative, afford
An ufefu' leffon.—Thefe the fleeting life

## AUTUMN.

Of vain fond man depict.—Kind Nature shows
To man, in the fair, vast variety
Of trees an' flow'rs, an emblem of himself.
His early infancy, his youth, an' age,
Are circumscrib'd within the narrow space
Of a short season—Man, of life no more,
Comparatively judg'd, enjoys, than do
The with'ring walys which we tread upon.
His being by *succession* is preserv'd—
And, " to be born—to die," of Nature is,
With humankind, the same as, in these woods,
To plant an acorn, hence, to fell an oak.—

The grove is still, an' not a twig is seen
To quiver with the breeze.—Throughout the warld
A sober calm precides.—Light fleeting clouds,
Acrofs th' unbounded ether, heave on high,
Shadowing with thin-wove robe the downward sun,
Who, through the trem'lous fleece, his milder rays
Shoots on the distant hills.—The time now is

For thofe, who love to walk, an' wonder, o'er
The realm of Nature, to diveft themfelves
Of carkin care ; an' frae the fordid crowd,
To feek to foar above the little fcenes
Of little things—to tread the peacefu' path
Of high improving Wifdom—and afpire,
Through a' the mazes of this *lower* walk,
The boundlefs fields of a fuperior world.
Thus, contemplative, through the fadden'd vale,
An' weather-beaten brake, aft let me gang,
Where, nor the mavis' nor the woodlark's voice,
Is now melodious heard.—Where, not a ftrain
Is fung, to chear the trav'ler on his way ;
Nor artlefs mufic chaunted—where the tribes
Of the gay feather'd people, dowy, fit,
Amang the tawny branches.—Where no voice
Awakens echo in the neighb'ring grove,
Save what the culver, fhooting frae the tap
O' the gray, airy elm, now utters, to
The dull difrobed wildernefs, in plaintive moan.

*There*

# AUTUMN.

There let me walk, amidst the dusky desart,
Where not a tree outlives the season's stroke—
Or, to the gloomy grotto carry me,
Where ghostly *figures* range—and *spectres* pale,
Tremendous, flow acrofs the dewy plain
Sweep silent—and, with voices low an' deep,
As the arch'd, hollow tomb, sad founding through
The dusky void, strike the reflecting mind
With philosophic force—and bids it look
Beyond mortality's *decaying* season,
Unto the verdure of eternal Spring.


The sun his chariot rolls, adown the sky,
In hurling haste.—The shorten'd day shuts in—
An' fogs, condensing in the gelid air,
Upo' the plains fall hoary—Humid even'
Along the western sky its vapors trails
In chilly train; an' to the pliant foot
O' plodding paffenger, the grassy path
Crumps sonorous.—The cattle, now, the fields

# AUTUMN.

Forsake, an' to the warmer *sheds* repair—
The flocks the cold an' wat'ry *summit* leave,
An' in the bosom of the silent hills
Convene, reclining, till the dawn o' day.
Where, in yon vale, the rushing river spreads—
Where, in yon marsh, the stagnant waters ooze—
An' where, in yonder glen, the gurgling rill
Loud murmurs in the breeze, the rolling mists,
Wi' a' their noxious matter, swim along,
An' cloud the atmosphere.—The silver'd moon,
Wi' shining horns, in fullest circle met,
Now frae the East, among the scatter'd clouds,
Holds on her way; an' o'er the silent world
Bespreads her wat'ry beams.—The distant rocks
Swell i'the shifting gleam; an' the still flood,
Compos'd an' calm, far on the sight reflects
The quiv'ring light.—Unclouded now, she rolls
Her upward course, in the precarious dress
Of borrow'd *glory*.—To the sun direct
She shows her spotted face, whereon are seen,

Dread

Dread *fights* of caverns deep, rocks, hills, an' dales,
An' mountains huge, on other mountains rais'd.
But foon the fable robes of gloomy night
O'erfpread the fky immenfe.—Now black an' deep
The clouds begin to rife, an' heav'n an' earth,
In the vaft fhade convolv'd, appear to meet.


'Tis night profound! The wide extended gloom,
Enwrapping earth an' feas, looks difmal to
The lonely voyager, afar remov'd
Frae weel-ken'd fhores, upo' the diftant waves
Of a tumultous ocean.—O'er his mind,
In this dread time of cloud-compelling ftorm,
What thoughts may come! His *all* being on the
    flood.
His fears arife wi' every coming furge—
Deadly defpair takes place of terror, and
Now, heedlefs of his fate, unto the winds
He yields the government of his frail bark.

# AUTUMN.

Tofs'd wi' the tempeft many joylefs hours,
At length the morning-ftar proclaims the day,
An' hopes arife, an' brighten on his foul.
Though to the *mariner* befet wi' ftorm,
The fhades of night fall difmal, yet, not to
The nightly *thief* they any terror bring—
Who rudely ranges thorough darkfome fcenes,
An' gleans his *harveft* frae *forbidden* fields.

Oh fee! in yonder pit, the carefu' bees,
In thoufands, frae their honied treafures drop;
An' heave in lteaps, amidft the fulph'rous death.
Ah! tell us, now, what evil have *they* done,
That they fhou'd frae the hand o' lordly *man*,
Deferve the blow tyrannical? Induftrious tribe!
Ye're not the *only* folk whom luxury,
An' rude voluptuoufnefs, have prey'd upon!
Teach us, ye haplefs people, by your death,
So to improve the fummer-hours of life,

That,

# AUTUMN.

That, when the gloomy veil upon *our* lot
Is overspread, and our last *Autumn* come,
We may drop frae our cells into the tomb,
Without or dread, or fear, right conscious, that
Unknowing of our end, we had improv'd
The sunny-minutes of our given day.

# WINTER.

# WINTER.

THUS far, my Muse, through the revolving year,
Has spun her song.—In gay, fresh-blushing Spring,
She wander'd through rich scenes of spreading flow'rs,
An' verdant meads.—In Summer's ardent blaze,
Among the bushy oaks she sat an' sang,
Befriended by the shade.—Through Autumn's gale,
Fraught with the perfumes of a plenteous year,
She brush'd with gladsome pace; and now, among
The wint'ry clouds, and through the rough domain
Of snows, an' howling storm, she tries to soar—
To raise her notes in concert with the wind;
An' make her cadence quaver with the flood.

He comes! sad Winter, on the winged blast,
Wi' a' his gloomy train, to crown the year.
Upo' his awfu' brow sit clouds an' hail,
In big-swoln gloomy pride—an' frae the skirts
Of his bedewed garment, vapors hang,
Fermenting the deep tempest with their pow'r;
An' glancing, grimly, through the brewing storm.


The sun now faintly o'er the sadden'd warld,
His yellow beams diffuses.—Not a flow'r
Throughout the gelid glebe is seen to show
Its beauty to the day—baith leaf an' stem
Droop wi' the nipping blast; and sink beneath
The rude oppression of the cold-clad year.
Black, broad, and deep, athwart the southern sky
The fogs arise, an' onward spread their force,
In hoary dew, diffusive o'er the plain—
Hence, cloudy storm, in sable robes begirt,
Obscures the visage of the azure heav'n.

Bleak

# WINTER.

Bleak Winter thus steps in, an' wi' a *gloom*
Frae wan oppressive eyes pervades the whole—
Shedding his killing pow'r, an' force malign,
Throughout the warld—Unto the theeked boose
The cattle, pinched by the surly day,
In haste repair; an' o'er fu' cribs o' strae,
Croon bold defiance to the howling blast.


The flocks, now, frae the snow-cap'd hills with
    speed
Down to the valleys trot, dowy an' mute;
An' round the hay-stack, crowding, pluck the stalks
O' wither'd *bent*, wi' gustfu' hungry bite.—
Now by the ingle-side the plowman sits,
Regardless o' the day, while, in the glebe
Condens'd, the bended cou'ter shows its sides,
Bespread with eating rust—an', nor the voice,
Nor whistle o' contentment, now is heard
Across the furrowed field.—Among the hills,
An' down the wat'ry marsh, the coming storm
                        Sughs

## WINTER.

Sughs awfu'—Up among the shelving cliffs
An' shaggy-browed mountains, loose an' gray,
The murm'ring rill sends forth a hollow moan,
Resounding frae ilk cave an' dreary dell.

Bauld Boreas, wi' his blasts, the dad o'storm,
Comes forth tempestuous, wrapp'd in dusky dress.
Forth frae the bleak Norwegian forests, tall,
An' Shetland's utmost cliff, the whizzing blast
Sweeps Southward.—On ilk airy mountain's top
The benty bushes, an' the breckans, yield
Unto the bending gust.—First, black an' loud,
Upo' the steady gale the tempest comes,
In sleet obscure, an' o'er the mingling skies,
Vapors an' clouds an' storm convening, dash
The craggy hills, an' shake the growling woods—
Congeal'd an' white the whirling tempest spreads
Its flaky pow'r; an' the unsightly plain
Groans underneath the deep'ning snowy load.
The sun no chearfu' ray darts through the gloom

# WINTER.

To hearten on his way the drooping fwain;
But, envelop'd in clouds of mirky hue,
Travels, unfeen, the journey of the day.
The tunelefs tenants o' the bufhy brae,
Sit dowy on ilk fpray, an' penfive eye
The branches, whit'ning by the fleecy fall.
Yet not thus idle a'—In ftack-yards fome
Induftrioufly pick up the fcatter'd ears,
That frae the fwingin *fupple* fpread afar.—
Some o'er the furrowed field hap haftily,
Chatt'ring doleful to the thick'ning ftorm;
An', crowding on the frefh-turn'd hillock, fkail,
Wi' eager nebs, the dufky frozen turf—
An' fome, lefs heedfu' o' the times, around
The cryftal pond delight to flutter throng.
Unto her hovel, dropping through, the fow,
Prefagefu' o' the blaft, the ftrae in *tates*
Right carefully collects.—Beneath the boughs
O' the wide-fpreading yew, hollow an' dry,
The dunghill feath'ry people, crowding, prefs,

Wi'

Wi' drooping tails, an' churm their penfive moan—
While by the hallan hid, the plow-boy ftands
Wi' fhining brofy vifage, keen, to pu'
The wily ftring o' the enfnaring trap,
Or chaff-deceiving *riddle*.—Urg'd by want,
Should an ill-fated fparrow venture on
The ftraw-ftrew'd guile, wi' heart uplifted, in
His hands he grafps the little fecklefs prey;
An', laughing, to his fellows rins wi' fpeed.


Wide o'er the warld, the flaky ftorm now fpreads
Its pinching pow'r.—The cattle, doom'd to brave
The Winter's blaft, among the diftant hills
Far 'hind frae bufh or biel, convening, ftand,
Tail-turned to the tempeft, licking, throng,
The fhiv'ring laggins o' their fcanty cuds.
The penfive fhepherd, frae his lowly cot,
Unto the hills walks carefu'.—Up amang
The lonely mountains, to the wreathed ftorm,
He fets his breaft, wi' ardent, fwafhing pith—

Impatient

# WINTER.

Impatient to find out his scatter'd flocks.
His faithfu' dog, the pride of tawdry tykes,
Between the banks o' Tweed, an' Crawford John,
O'er heaps o' *tempest* brushing, round the hills,
An' frae the distant glen, wi' care, compels
The lonely tip, at whose dun shaggy sides
The ratt'ling ishogles, depending, skim
The snowy deluge.—Gather'd on the plain,
The clam'rous, bleating warld is heard afar.


Ye gen'rous swains, unto that race be kind—
'Tis worth your care.—Let not the deep'ning *drift*,
Over your charge prevail.—Draw out now, frae
Your care-collected store, the balmy hay,
An' fill their *pens*.—Safe on the airy dale
The helpless nation lodge; and, ear' an' late,
Supply their hunger-calls, wi' food at will.
Below the tempest safe, now, 'tis your care
To watch them well, lest in the snowy wreath
They smother'd fall; for, frae the blust'ring North

Fu' aft is seen the tossing storm to come,
Sweeping the wint'ry bent, an', to the vale,
Hurling the drifted load, till, with the hills,
Deep cleughs an' caverns rife, an' i'the air
High glist'ning, point their summits to the sky.


Keen blows the wind; an' frae the burthen'd fells,
The powd'ry storm's uplifted.—Through the air,
The rushing tempest wafts, frae hill to hill;
(A joyless sight to the wayfaring swain)
Involving woods an' rivers, beasts an' men,
In the wild fury of the whirling blast.


'Tis even'—the atmosphere serene an' clear—
And the rude strength o' the beclouded day
Now overpast.—Unto far distant climes,
The snowy tempest has its force withdrawn;
An', in the warm recesses o' the South,
Is sunk, the fury o' the fleecy warld.—
The feather'd nation now is hush'd to rest—

Beneath

# WINTER.

Beneath the thatched eave, the sparrow takes
Her dull *repose*.—The mavis, sad an' mute,
Close in the brake conceal'd, upon a twig,
Outsits the dreary night; an' on the top
O' the high-tow'ring elm, the soaring kite,
By wint'ry famine tame, now fearless sits;
An' drooping, dozes till the dawn of day.
'Tis silence all—e'en not a *voice* is heard,
Throughout the calm profound, save, what the owl,
Wailing the wint'ry tide, does frae her bow'r
Send sadden'd, forth.—The delug'd wilderness,
Now in the sad an' solemn midnight-hour,
Emits its wild inhabitants.—Across
The trackless plain, frae foodless forests led,
To seek for sustenance, the timid hare,
Unto the kail-yard stens.—Now bold by want,
She fearless ranges through the orchards wide,
Mumping the juicy bark, frae twig to stem.
Thither she comes to claim her little share,
Though in the dark bestow'd, of what kind Heav'n

Affigns his creatures.—Let not now thy hand
Be lifted up to flay; nor, of neceffity
Take the advantage.—When, at early dawn,
Wi' feeding tir'd, fhe to the *wild* returns,
Purfue her to her hill, or ferny haunt;
An', with thy dog, take of the *fport* thy fill.


In this fad dreary time, when a' the warld,
Drowfy an' dumb, lies funk in fleep profound,
Let me contemplate on the gloomy hour;
An' fecretly affociate with the ftorm.


Hence a' difcordant thoughts! a' watchfu' cares!
Ye bufy-meddling fenfes a' begone!
An' let pure *Meditation* reign, throughout
My cogitative pow'rs.—Where in this quiet
An' filent, fleep-feiz'd hour, are to be found
The flutt'ring variety of cheating life?
Where are the train of fpeculations falfe,
Which, with the fun, inceffant rife an' fet?—

Now

# WINTER.

Now wrap'd in death-like flumbers, the vain warld,
Without diftinction, refts.—The cares of life,
In light an' airy vifions are diffolv'd;
An' brown-fac'd toil, for a fhort feafon eas'd,
Enjoys the comfort of found fweet repofe.


Thou Power Supreme! whofe might no weaknefs knows—
Whofe all-obferving eye, the great domain
Of Heav'n an' Earth pervades—whofe fight, the dark
An' gloomy fhades of night cannot obfure—
Teach me, as I admire thy wond'rous works,
To know thy goodnefs.—While the ringing blaft,
Againft my cafement beats—while fleet an' fnaw,
In wreathed ftorm, lies thick on ilka hill,
May I, baith bien an' warm, within my cot,
Look heedfu' to the times.—May I be taught
In Summer's heat, an' Winter's nipping cold,
In *fun* an' *fhade*, to know thy works an' Thee!

## WINTER.

The dawn looks in, an' to their diſtant haunts
The prowling warld retire.—The artfu' tod,
Wi' hen-rooſt plunder fraught, unto his *hold*,
In wild bewild'ring glen, ſcours faſt, ſweeping
The ſnowy hillock as he bears along
The fatted capon, o'er his ſhouther flung.
Sated wi' herbage ſweet, the artleſs hare
The kail-yard leaves, an', to the whinny brae,
Haps, heedfu'.—Now, the voice of chanticleer
The hamlet wakes; an', frae his lowly bed
The ruſtic ſwain arous'd, unto the bent,
Through bogs an' buſhes flouncing, preſſes faſt,
The *downy mumper*, eager, to deſtroy.
To trace her footſteps more exactly, he
About his garden walks, eying with care
Each ſecret wicket, to his bow-kail ſtems.
Great he finds the *warping* to have been,
Upo' each plat, as if the hirpling race
Had met in general concourſe.—Frae the hedge,
At length, the freſh-made footſteps he deſcrys,

To lead unto the hill.—Glad at the fair
Diſtinction, wi' his gun, an' ſturdy tyke,
He hurries ſoftly, by the tract conducted,
Unto the buſhy ſummit.—Meanwhile, in
The ferny covert, ſnug, poor maukin ſits,
Undreaming o' the faithleſs ſnaw; chewing
Her well-repleniſh'd cud.—Now, cloſe upon
Her ſnow-cap'd haunt, the rude purſuer comes,
Eager, an' watchfu', leſt his crumping tread
Should her untimely rouſe.—Wi' heedfu' ſtep
He rounds ilk buſh, cautious, an' ſtarting aft',
Should at his feet a ſcared yorlin bir;
Or icicle drop frae the bended twig,
Wi' fiſſling din, amang the leafleſs bri'rs.
Led by the tract diſtinct, upo' his prey,
Brown, latent 'neath the ſtorm, he *caſts* his eyes—
His heart's baith fear'd an' fain.—Faſt frae his
  lug,
The thund'ring *charge* is ettled; and, amain,
The death-ſtruck victim bounces frae her feat,

By leaden impulſe—and, the cruſted drift
Beſprinkles wi' her mangled crimſon life.


Leſs barb'rous ſome bruſh rackleſs through the brake;
An', frae her ſecret *form*, the prey beſtirs—
Whence, to the hills, by yelping dogs purſu'd,
She nimbly ſtens out o'er the heaps o' ſnow.


The ſun his yellow beams begins to ſpread,
Upo' the mountain tops.—Now, far an' near,
Frae hill to diſtant dale, is heard the thud
O' the divulſive flail.—The huſbandman,
Ariſing wi' the day, unto the plain
Faſt bears the tedded ſtrae; an', 'fore his *care*,
Dowy, an' rowtin dolefu', lays in heaps
The huſky provender.—Frae diſtant groves,
Black trains of rooks, clam'rous an' hungry, urge
Their morning flight; an' 'mang the crumping herd,
Crowd fearleſs, picking the thin ſcatter'd grain.
Urg'd too, by want, the couring partricks, from

The

# WINTER.

The thorny cover steal, an', with the rooks
Tumultuous, quietly mix, an' 'midst the store
Of strae an' chaff dispers'd, promisc'ous, scrape.

The day is risen to meridian height;
An' the deep-drifted eaves, touch'd by the warmth,
Upo' the ragged pavement patter, fast.
The shorten'd day draws downward; and, unto
Their separate retreats, the feather'd warld
Again repair.—Now, through the blue serene,
The forcive pow'r o' the concocting frost
Comes snell an' keen.—The azure arched heav'n,
With stars innumerable, is cover'd o'er;
Which, twinkling through the aerial void immense,
In fair majestic show, adorn the sky;
An' ceaseless speak much harmony divine.

Now frae the hill, unto the tufted cot,
The carefu' swain, in straw-boots shod, returns—
His kind officious wife, the ingle stirs;

His

An' brings him veſtments warm.—His children round
Him toddle, an' contend, wi' buſtling might,
Who ſhall the happy welcome utter firſt;
Who ſhall ſhare moſt of the paternal ſmile.


"Keen blows the wind, an' piercing is the cold"
By potent energy, frae his bleak ſtores,
*Froſt* ſends his arrows forth—his ſecret pow'r
Invading all, an' o'er the warld immenſe,
Diffuſing, breathes his cloſe arreſting pith;
An' water, earth, an' air intenſely binds.
The purling ſtream leſs gurgles—an' the film,
Borne by the boiling eddy, now no more
Upo the ſurface wheels, but, to the bank,
An' round the pointed rocks, firmly cements
A cryſtal ſheet faſt ſeiz'd throughout the pool.
Loud rings the frozen glebe—an' to the ear,
The clogged wheel o' the way-faring wain
Grates, diſmal.—To th' oppreſſive haſty tread
O' th' benighted trav'ler the hollow plain

Sounds

# WINTER.

Sounds sadd'ning frae afar—while, frae ilk pole,
The azure firmament, intensely keen,
Orbs infinite displays.—Incessant, through
The lengthen'd night serene, the stiff'ning force
O' the enclasping cold fa's fast upon
The whitened warld—till bright *day*, at last
Starts frae his southern couch, wi' joyless look,
Upo' the sounding fells.—The morn', again,
Calls forth the shepherd to his wonted hill;
An' bids the drooping cottager repair
Unto his daily toil, to try to earn,
In snow, an' harden'd storm, his daily food.

Now, rude the wonders of the *wild* appear,
Involv'd in drifted tempest, fast congeal'd.
The various labor o' the night intense,
In dripping cave, an' murm'ring water-fall,
Looks rough an' hoary, to the rising day.
Frae thatched eaves the icicles depend,
In glitt'ring show—an' the once bick'ring stream,

                                       Imprison'd

Imprison'd by the ice, low-growling, runs,
Below the cryftal pavement.—Wi' the dawn,
The wild-goofe wings her way, frae frozen lakes,
In fearch o' fuftenance in tepid fens.
The fnipe, rous'd by the early traveller,
Starts frae the flimy drain ; and, to the fpring,
Wide fmoking with the fun, now waubles faft.
The teal, infenfate to her haplefs fate,
At fetting fun, amidft the loofen'd ice
Her ftation takes.—The lapper'd lake, 'ere morn,
Cementing, firm, frae fhore to fhore, involves
Her *lucken* feet, faft frozen in the flood.
Now to the open fprings, amidft the fhade
Of tow'ring fpeargrafs, in the filent marfh,
The wild-duck bends her flight.—There, frae the view
Of tyrannous man conceal'd, fhe feeds fecure,
Upo' the graffy blade—her only ftore
That may furvive the ftorm.—Be it thy care,
Fond Sporfman ! while the gloomy veil of night

Thy

Thy purpofe fhades, to reach the cover'd bank,
Which over-looks the pool—an' while, at dawn,
The quaiking tribe advances, point your *piece*,
Wi' flug well charg'd; an' rake the wheeling ftring,
Frae van to rear, wi' the rude rankling death.

The fun, ftill urging onward in his courfe,
Again our region bleffes.—Now, afar,
Among the fnow-clad hills, the village fmokes;
An' a' the jovial fons of honeft mirth,
Wi' gladfome hearts, bid welcome to the day.

Forth to the frozen lake, on frolic keen,
The youthfu' fwains repair.—A medley *throng*,
On various fports intent, hither refort;
An' mixing in the band of focial life,
Fondly conveen'd, upo' the river crowd.—
*Old age* is here an idle *looker-on*,
On revelry, in which it once did join.
E'en infants, here, mix with the multitude,
        Utt'ring

Utt'ring their puerile clamour, to the skies.
Some shoot the icy fragments.—To the goal,
Some hurl the polish'd pebble.—Some the top,
Fast whirling frae their thumbs, whip dext'rously—
An' some, bold, frae the crushed bank dart on,
String after string, the sleek well-polish'd *slide*.
Hither, the manly *youth*, in jovial bands,
Frae ev'ry hamlet swarm.—Swift as the wind
Some sweep, on sounding skates, smoothly along,
In dinsome clang, circling a thousand ways,
Till the wide crystal pavement, bending, rairs,
Frae shore to shore, by th' rush o' madden'd joy.
On sledges some hurl rapidly along,
Eager, an' turning oft' to 'scape the flaws,
An' dang'rous chinks, the wind an' sun have made.
But, manliest of all ! the vig'rous *youth*,
In bold contention met, the channelstane,
The bracing engine of a Scottish arm,
To shoot wi' might an' skill.—Now, to the lake,
At rising sun, with hopes of conquest flush'd,

The

The armed heroes meet.—Frae dale to doon
The salutation echoes—and, amain,
The baubee tofs'd, wha shall wi' ither fight,
The cap'ring combatants the war commence—
Hence, loud, throughout the vale, the noise is heard,
Of thumping rocks, an' loud bravadoes' roar.

God profper long the hearty friends
 Of honeft pleafures. all ;
A mighty *curling* match once did
 At C*****w**k befal.


To hurl the channelftane wi' fkill,
 Lanfloddan took his way ;
The child that's yet unborn will fing,
 The curling of that day.


The champion of Ullifdale
 A broad rafh aith did make,
His pleafure, near the Cam'ron ifle,
 Ae winter's day to take.


Bold Ben o' Tudor fent him word,
 He'd match him at the fport.
The Chief o' Ken, on hearing this,
 Did to the ice refort.

# WINTER.

Wi' channelſtanes, baith glib an' ſtrong,
    His army did advance—
Their *crampets* o' the truſty ſteel,
    Like bucklers broad did glance.


A band, wi' beſoms, high uprear'd,
    Weel made o' broom the beſt,
Before them, like a moving wood,
    Unto the combat preſs'd.


The gallant gameſters briſkly mov'd
    To meet the daring fae—
On Monday they had reach'd the lake,
    By breaking of the day.


The chieftains muſter'd on the ice,
    Right eager to begin—
Their channelſtanes, by ſpecial care,
    Where a' baith ſtout an' keen.

Their rocks they hurled up the rink—
　　Ilk to *bring in* his hand—
An' hill an' valley, dale an' doon,
　　Rang wi' the ardent band.


Glenbuck upo' the *cockee* stood—
　　His merry men drew near—
Quoth he, Bentudor promifed
　　This morn' to meet me here.


But if I thought he would not come—
　　We'd join in focial play.
With that, the *leader* of the ice,
　　Unto Glenbuck did fay


Lo, yonder does Bentudor come—
　　His men wi' crampets bright—
Twelve channelftanes, baith hard an' fmooth,
　　Come rolling in our fight.

All

All chósen rocks of Mulloch heugh,
    Faſt by the tow'ring Screel—
Then tye your *crampets*, Glenbuck cries—
    Prepare ye for the ſpeal.

And now with me, choice men of Ken,
    Your curling ſkill diſplay—
For never was their *curler* yet,
    Of village or of brae,

That e'er wi' channelſtane did come,
    But if he would ſubmit
To *hand* to *nieve* I'd pledge this crag,
    I ſhould his *winner* hit.

Bentudor, like a warrior bold,
    Came foremoſt o' them a'—
A beſom on his ſhouther flung;
    On's hans twa mittens bra.

An' with him forth came Tullochfern;
    An' Tom o' Broomyshaw—
Stout Robert o' Hefton, Ratcliff, and
    Young John o' Fotheringhaw.

An' wi' the laird o' Cairnyhowes,
    A *curler* guid an' true,
Good Ralph o' Titherbore, an' Slacks—
    Their *marrows* there are few.

Of Fernybank needs muft I fpeak,
    As ane of aged fkill.
Simon of Shots, the nephew bold
    Of Cairny on the hill.

With brave Glenbuck came *curlers* twelve—
    All dext'rous men of Dee.
Robin o' Mains, Clim o' the Cleugh,
    An' fam'd Montgomery.

Gamewell

Gamewell the brisk, of Napplehowes,
    A valiant blade is he.
Harry o' Thorn, Gib o' the Glen,
    The stoutest o' the three.


An' the young heir of Birnyholm,
    Park, Craigs, Lamb o' the lin—
Allan of Airds, a *sweeper* good;
    An' Charley o' Lochfin.


Bentudor a Riscarrel crag,
    Twice up the ice hurl'd he,
Good sixty cloth-yards, and a span,
    Saying, " so long let it be."


It pleas'd them a'—Ilk then wi' speed,
    Unto his weapon flew—
First, Allan o' Airds his whinstane *rock*,
    Straight up the *white ice* drew.

" *A good beginning!*" cries Glenbuck—
  Slacks fidging at the fight,
Wi's bra *blue-cap,* lent Airds a fmack;
  Then roared out " *good night!*"

Next Robin o' Mains, a *leader* good,
  Clofe to the witter drew—
Ratcliff went by, an' 'caufe he mifs'd,
  Pronounc'd the ice untrue.

Gib o' the Glen, a noble *herd,*
  Behind the *winner* laid—
Then Fotheringhaw, a fidelin fhot,
  Clofe to the *circle* play'd.

Montgom'ry, mettlefu', an' fain,
  A racklefs ftroke did draw;
But mifs'd his aim, an' 'gainft the *herd,*
  Dang frae his *clint* a flaw.

With that ſtepp'd forward Tullochfern,
    An' (ſaying to hit, he'd try)
A leal ſhot ettled at the cock,
    Which ſhov'd the *winner* by.

Clim o' the Cleugh, on ſeeing that,
    Sten'd forth, an' frae his knee,
A ſlow ſhot drew, wi' muckle care,
    Which ſettled on the *tee*.

Ralph, vexed at the fruitleſs play,
    The cockee butted faſt—
His ſtane being glib, to the loch-en',
    Cloſe by the witter paſt.

Stout Robert o' Heſton, wi' his broom,
    Came ſtepping up wi' might—
Quoth he, " my *Abbey-burn-fit*
    Shall win the *ſpeal* this night.

With that brisk Gamewell, up the rink,
   His well *mill'd* rock did hurl—
Which rubbing Ratcliff on the *cheek*,
   Around the cock did twirl.

Now stepp'd a noted gamester forth,
   Fernybank was his name—
Wha said, he would not have it told
   At C\*\*\*\*\*w\*\*k, for shame;

That e'er the chief o' Ken should bear
   The palm of victory—
Then heezing his Kilmarnock hood,
   Unto the *cock* drew he.

The *stanes* wi' muckle martial din,
   Rebounding frae ilk shore,
Now thick, thick, thick, each other chas'd,
   An' up the rink did roar.

They

They clofed faft on every fide—
    A *port* could fcarce be found—
An' many a broken channelftane
    Lay fcatter'd up an' down.


" Show me the winner," crys Glenbuck;
    " An' a' behind ftan' aff;"
Then rattled up the rocking crag,
    An' ran the port wi' *life*.


Bentudor flung his bonnet by,
    An' took his ftane wi' fpeed—
Quoth he, " my lads, the day is ours"—
    *Their* chance is paft remead.


Syne hurlin through the crags o'Ken,
    Wi' *inrings*, nice an' fair,
He ftruck the *winner* frae the cock,
    A lang claith-yard, an' mair.

The fpeal did laft frae nine forenoon,
    Till fetting 'o' the fun—
For when the hern fcraich'd to her tree,
    The combat fcarce was done.


Thus did Bentudor an' Glenbuck,
    Their curling conteft end.
They met baith merry i'the morn'—
    At night they parted friends.

# WINTER.

The sportive *field* is o'er.—Now, friendly, all
Conveened o'er a bowl of nect'rous juice,
Recount the fam'd achievements o' the day—
The song goes round.—Among the jovial sons
O' health an' peace, true mirth is melody.
Regardless of, or consonance or voice, the catch, the
    glee,
The martial tale is sung—an' frae the mouths
O' the concording company, applause abounds.
The laugh, the roar, the mirthfu' story, round
The wakefu' table spread.—The banter too,
For eminence in curling pow'r an' skill,
Rings through the lighted dome.—Again, the hard,
The well-contested *speal* is called up—
The wide-spread *table* to the rink is turn'd;
An' bowls an' bottles, implements of *war*.
Here stands the *winner* by a bottle hid,
Immoveable, save by a nice *inring*—
*There* stands the *tee*—up through this *port* he came,
Wi' a' his might—on *this* he gently rubb'd—

                            On

On *that* he brak an *egg*—from *that* to *this*,
From *this* to *that*, thump, thump, amidſt the
    thrang;
At length the winner ſtruck, wi' mettled ſmack;
An' ſent *him* birling up aboon the *fire*.


Since jovial thus, the ſocial ſons of mirth,
The wint'ry minutes paſs—be it *my* lot,
In ſome ſnug corner of my native land,
Unknowing, or *ſervility* or *wealth*,
Far frae the buſy warld, remote to dwell;
Where, loud the ſounding ſkate, upo' the lake,
Re-echoes frae ilk ſhore—where hurling ſledge,
Upo' the icy pavement, boundeth far;
An' where the channelſtane loud roaring, makes
The hamlet hynd depreſs'd wi' penſive cares,
Forget his every trouble, in his joy.
There, in ſome quiet retirement, would I paſs
The Winter's gloomy days, wi' ſocial friends
O' ſterling wit an' jeſt.—With them I'd join

# WINTER.

In a' the various scenes o' rural mirth,
An' rural joy.—With them, o' pliant soul,
I would of Nature's boundless province sing—
Admiring still the Season's gradual change;
An' each fair object through the varied year.

The moon, full orbed, o'er the *lift* serene,
Slides brightly.—Now the wakefu' *village* swarms
Upo' the sheeted puddle, sportive, in
The bond of social merriment, promiscuous, met.
Some set astride on stools, are push'd along
Upo' the floored flosh—while some on stanes,
Frae the smooth top o' the incrusted brae,
Adown the slipp'ry surface swiftly glide.
The rustic swain within his cottage sits;
An' rousing up the ingle, bids the hand
Of industry go on.—The *eident* lass
Draws frae the teazing comb, the *fined* fleece—
The spinner turns the wheel wi' nimble hand—

The

The chuffy callan in the corner leans,
Peeling hempen ftalks.—The goblin ftory,
By hear-fay only often handed down,
Is fondly told, till fuperftitious fear
Pervades the firefide, an' horror creeps
Through ilk alarmed breaft, involving e'en
The *teller* in the terror, by his tale.
Or frequent in the lighted chamber, they
In rural mirth, by fcrape o' fiddle rous'd,
Their gambols play.—The *bumpkin* brifk, is up—
The floor *conducted*; an' wi' nimble heels,
To the tune *Shawntrews*, the hornpipe is cut.
Ruftic fimplicity in pleafing jeft,
Flows frae ilk fhepherd's tongue.—The laugh, the
    joke,
In much good humour, round the circle fpread;
An' frae the dozing maid, guardlefs, alone,
Is fnatch'd the hafty kifs.—Thus, the dull hours,

O'

O' winter-gloom, glide on, jocund an' gay;
An' love, refponfive, crowns the ftormy night.


The bauld, keen-biting force of Boreas, by
The bluft'ring South is blunted.—Now, the froft,
Refolving to a thaw, through mead an' dale,
Runs trickling to the burn.—The mountains now,
Unto the morning fun, their airy fides
Show fpotted.—And, the drizzling heavy clouds,
Adown ilk valley fpread.—Soft fleet defcends—
An' rain, faft rufhing frae the vap'rous *lift*,
Drives through the air; an' 'gainft the fnowy cliff,
Dafhes wi' drenching pith.—The drifted glens,
Sunk by the foft'ning zephyrs, an' the rills,
Long bound wi' frozen tempeft, now begin
To trickle, gurgling, through the loofen'd ftorm.
The deep'ning rivers o'er their verges fwell,
Impetuous, bearing on the madden'd ftream
The icy fragments, crafhing awfu' o'er
Each rocky fall, unto the briny main.

         Now

Now to the rifen day, the wat'ry world
Its delug'd face prefents.—The fnow-fed ftreams,
Though woods an' valleys fwell; an' the wide
    plain,
Loud fughing frae afar, a fullen flood
Sends rufhing to the deep, a thoufand ways,
Leaving the grafslefs braes, a flimy wafte.


Stern Winter now, upo' the fadden'd fields,
His laft grim *look* prefents.—How dreary 'neath
His flatt'ning rigid pow'r, the vegetable,
An' tunefu' warlds lie!—Dread devaftation,
Throughout the wide domain, horror extends,
An' fweeps triumphant, o'er the vanquifh'd year.


The fun, more potent, temperates the clods;
An' Spring peeps cautious on the biely braes.
The hufbandman walks lightly o'er the glebe,
The plough-tail glad to touch.—The new-born
    year
                                            Begets

Begets rejoicing in the Shepherd's breast,
While on he plods, his wonted hills among,
Collecting to the fold, his scatter'd flock.

Now frae her storm-bound port, the trading
   bark
Forth launches to the deep.—The coming sun
Gladdens ilk heart, wi' his enliv'ning pow'r—
Recruits the waned visage o' the year;
An' bids the springing world smile again.

## FINIS.

LIKE mony mae, wi' what they write,
Unto the *heap* I've caſt my *mite*—
But let not any coof, through ſpite,
     Condemn the thing.
For Nature ſaid ſhe wou'd indite,
     If I cou'd ſing.


My tip-horn ſyne, I loudly tooted;
An' ca'd the Muſe, that was ſure-footed;
An' bade her gallop, nimble-cooted,
     Through thick and thin—
Her *tittas* clap'd their hips an' hooted,
     " Ah hole ahin !"


Yet ne'er a ane o' them ſhe heeded,
But over hills an' dales faſt ſpeeded—
She ken'd right well, that what I needed,
     Wi' a' that buſtle,
Was, what nane o' them ever dreamed—
     A boortree whuſtle.

The pipe procur'd—an' wi' 't contented—
Fu' faſt the ſide o' Screel I ſklented—
My ſaul wi' verra joy was ſtented
                When, at the ſummit,
I to my lips the t'.ing preſented,
                That I could *bum* it.


Tir'd wi' the ſteep, an' ſomething dizzy,
I hunker'd down, ſae did the hizzy—
We then began to be ſae buſy,
                As ne'er was like—
As on I wrote, ſhe look'd ſae cozy,
                It gar'd me fyke—


She bade me look frae pole to pole;
An' ſing the wide amazing *whole*—
But, quoth I, laſſie, do but thole
                My quill a wee—
'Tween John o' Groats, an' Bogle-Hole,
                Eneugh I ſee.

Well pleas'd baith, wi' riggs an' bogs,
Meads, dales, an' braes, an' shady scrogs;
An' dinsome clang o' boys an' dogs,
     I on did scribble—
We gied our pows the tither shog,
     To make it dribble.


Spring in our minds we circumveen'd,
Adorned like a Pathian Queen,
Wi' flow'rets lovely to be seen;
     A beauteous train—
With moon-light dancers on the green,
     A' friskin fain.


Through Summer's ardent walks we trod,
'Mang burning stanes, an' melting clods—
The brown burn-brae, an' scorched sod,
     Our notes rehears'd—
Which made us say, " 'Tis e'en right odd
     To write in verse."

       Through

Through Autumn's walks, o' bushy pines—
O' yellow corn, an' ripen'd vines—
We brush'd our way—yet, laith to tine
    Amang the sprouts
Of luscious grapes, an' peaches fine,
    The passage out.


'Mang Winter's snaws, turn'd almost doited,
I swagger'd forth—but near han' stoited—
The Muse, at that, grew capernoited;
    An' ca'd me bumble—
Then on my doup, I straightway cloited,
    Saying " Miss, your humble."

# AN EPISTLE
## TO
# WILLIAM BURNEY,
## A
## BROTHER POET.

SEE, Willy! thou poetic wag—
Booted and spur'd, I'm on my nag—
Come mount, an' with thee bring the bag
    O' thy *best swatches*—
Nane that can o' a *new coat* brag,
    Will boast of *patches*.


I'm on my *round* to take in *orders*—
Wha *fastest* rides does aft *least* forder—
Therefore, ere we shall reach the *border*,
    May be *your* Muse
Shall see *my* poney out of order,
    For lack o' shoes.

      But

But I'll jog on as I've begun;
An' speak my *quarters* with the fun—
Though a' the warld shou'd o' 't mak fun;
    An' ca' me coof—
Whene'er I shoot wi' my *air gun*
     'Tis ay aff loof.


If with moors, mires, an' morasses,
Our *poneys* tire, we'll then take *asses*—
A prentice cadie o' Parnassus,
    Upo' an' erran',
Must not regard it, how he passes,
     If wi' a *warran'*.


So come awa, my winsome Billy—
Apply the spurs unto thy filly—
The road at best they say is *hilly*—
    But up ilk steep,
Where we can't *walk* it fair an' fully
     I' faith we'll *creep*.

[ 183 ]

But I'll jog on as I've begun;
I'll speak my quarrel with the sun,
Though in the early Bounds of Light;
And then I'll fairly bid good night.

Whate'er I think we may all grin,
"Tis ay all for't

If with accent, infers a contradiction as with
Only if 'tis so, we'll then take it—
A certain case of

I'll say not regard it, like the publick as
He will

Bawl'd,
And

Rough

# GLOSSARY.

### A.

ABOON, *above*
Aff-loof, *off-hand, extempore*
Aught, *eight*

### B.

Ba's, *balls, heaps*
Bass, *a place in the East of Scotland*
Baith, *both*
Ban, *curse*
Beltan, *Whitsuntide*
Bengairn, *a hill adjoining Screel*
Bentudor, *a hill adjoining Bengairn*
Beetle, *a wooden instrument to mash potatoes*
Bienly, *well, happily*
Biggin, *building*
Bill, *bull*
Birny, *covered with singed heath*
Birslin, *scorching*
Bluidy-fingers, *fox-glove*
Bleezing, *blazing, flaming*
Bonny, *lovely, pretty*
Booricks, *shepherds' huts*

Boortree, *wild alder*
Bowkail, *cabbages*
Brae, *rising ground*
Brainge, *confused haste*
Brattle, *run quickly*
Brekans, *fern*
Breeks, *breeches*
Bruilie, *bruising*
Bumbee-bykes, *wildbees' nests*
Bum, *backside*
Bummels, *wild bees*
Bumble, *blunderer*
Buntlin, *blackbird*
Burn, *a rivulet*

### C.

Caller, *cool*
Canny, *heedful*
Caper, *frisk, dance*
Capernoited, *angry, impatient*
Carkin, *scratching*
Chap, *knock*
Chirtin, *confining laughter*
Chink, *money*
Churm, *tune, sing*
Clachan, *village*
Claff,

# GLOSSARY.

Claff, *cliff*
Clocks, *beetles*
Clock, *hatch*
Cloited, *squatted, sat down*
Cluds, *clouds, multitudes*
Cluthers, *heaps, crowds*
Colly, *a dog*
Coof, *blockhead*
Corback, *roof of an house*
Cour, *ly squat*
Cowing, *cutting*
Cowan, *not a free mason*
Craig, *rock, the neck*
Croon, *hum, sing*
Crouse, *courageous*
Cutes, *ancle bones*

### D.

Dee. *This river issues from a lake of the same name; and, after a meandring course among the hills, joins the river Ken, a few miles below the town of New Galloway, where it forms a lake, called Loch Ken, above eight miles in length; falling thence, a short space, it forms an island; on the south end of which, stands the celebrated Castle Trief—there, uniting, it takes a S. W. course, and falls into the sea at Kirkcudbright*
Dights, *wipes*
Donsy, *unfortunate*
Doos, *pigeons*

Dorty, *haughty, nice*
Doup, *bottom, backside*
Dowy, *lowspirited, melancholy*
Draps, *falls*
Duddy, *ragged*
Dunner, *thundering noise*

### E.

Eerie brow, *frightened, wild countenance*
Eild, *age*
Erts, *urges, prompts*

### F.

Farley, *wonder*
Fash'd, *troubled, concerned*
Feckless, *weak*
Fell, *rocky hill*
Fit, *foot*
Flosh, *swamp*
Foggy, *soft downy grass*
Forbears, *forefathers*
Forfairn'd, *fatigued, frightened, confused*
Frae, *from*
Fremmit, *stranger, foe*
Fur, *furrow*
Fumert, *a pole-cat*
Fykes, *fidges*

### G.

Gab, *mouth, muzzle*
Gang, *go, walk*
Gar, *make, oblige*
Gimmers, *ewes*
Girn, *grin, to complain*

Glaiket,

# GLOSSARY. 187

Glaiket, *wanton*
Gled, *kite*
Gleg, *quickfighted*
Glens, *dells*
Glent, *twinkle*
Glowrin, *gazing, flaring*
Gopinfus, *handfuls*
Gouk, *cuckoo*
Gowan, *a flower*
Gully, *knife*
Gumsheon, *knowledge, sense*

## H.

Haffet, *forehead, the temples*
Hallan, *door*
Hallion, *a clown*
Hayes, *a dance by three persons in the figure* 8
Heezy, *conveyance*
Hefts, *lifts up, carries*
Heght, *heavy fall*
Hillan, *hillock*
Hinny-crock, *honey-cup*
Hirples, *limps*
Hoke, *dig*
Hole-ahin, *term of reproach*
Hoody, *crow*
Hoolets, *owls*
Hostin, *coughing*
Howes, *valleys*
Hurdies, *posteriors*

## I.

Jaws, *waves*
Jazy, *wig*

Ingle, *fire*
Jumper, *a boring-iron*

## K.

Keaws, *daws*
Keek, *look*
Kemp'd, *striven*
King-hood, *great gut*
Kinkin, *vomiting*
Kimmers, *witches*
Kir, *wanton*
Kirn, *the feast called Harvest-home*
Knowe, *little hill, a hillock*

## L.

Laggin, *bottom*
Lapper'd, *encrusted, thickened*
Leal, *honest, true*
Lift, *sky, heaven*
Limmer, *a term of reproach*
Lin, *glen, or dell*
Linties, *linnets*
Lochan, *small lake*,
Loof, *hollow of the hand*
Lowin, *blazing*
Luckies, *old women*
Lucken, *web-footed*
Lugs, *ears*
Lunner, *smart stroke*
Lyart, *spotted, of various hues*

## M.

Mair, *more*
Mawkin, *hare*
Mavis, *thrush*

Meltit,

Meltit, *meal, repaft*
Midges, *a kind of flies*
Mifcaed, *nicknamed*
Mifrid, *revelled*
Moudy, *mole*
Muckle, *much, great*
Mun, *spoon*

### N.

Nae, *no*
Napple, *a sweet wild root*
Nappy, *nut-brown ale*
Neb, *bill*
Noofly, *handsomely*

### O.

Ony, *any*

### P.

Padder'd, *beaten, trodden*
Paddock, *frog*
Peghing, *breathing haftily*
Pellucks, *porpoises*
Penches, *entrails*
Pet piats, *tame magpies*
Pingle-pan, *tin pot*
Plodded, *walked at random*
Plumrocks, *primroses*
Pows, *heads*
Powheads, *tadpoles*
Prie, *tafte*
Purn, *reel of yarn*

### R.

Racklefs, *regardlefs*
Rair, *report*

Reeking, *smoaking*
Riddle, *fieve*
Riggin, *roof, back*
Rin, *run*
Routh, *plenty*
Rowt, *bellow, lowe*

### S.

Saig, *bullock*
Saugh trees, *withies*
Scarrow, *faint light*
Scour, *to move fwiftly*
Screel, *This mountain is fituated in the Stewarty of Kirkcudbright; from its fummit there is an extenfive profpect; it commands an uninterrupted view of the Solway Frith, from the Mull of Galloway to the River Nith—and of the Englifh fhore, from Carlifle to St. Bee's Head, with the Ifle of Man diftinctly. To the northward, inland, the view is terminated by the hills of Cree, diftant about forty miles.*
Screed, *roar*
Scrimpit, *fcarce meafure*
Scroggy, *bufhy*
Selchs, *feals*
Shangin, *a cleft ftick put to a dog's tail*
Shoots, *bloffoms*
Sic, *fo, fuch*
Sinny, *funny*

Skep,

# GLOSSARY. 189

Skep, *hive*
Sklentin, *oblique*
Skraich, *screech*
Sleugh, *slough*
Snoddest, *smoothest*
Sock, *part of a plough*
Sod, *turf*
Sonsy, *well-favoured, sweet, mild*
Sosses, *falls heavily*
Spae, *foretell*
Spartle, *jerk, leap*
Spate, *heavy rain, a flood*
Spaul, *limb*
Speels, *climbs*
Spleuchan, *pouch*
Sploiting, *spouting, squirting*
Spool, *shuttle*
Spruce, *smart*
Squintin, *leering*
Stane, *stone*
Starved, *satiated*
Sten, *leap*
Stoited, *staggered*
Stoor, *dust*
Strae, *straw*
Streaw, *a shrew mouse*
Sugh, *noise*
Supple, *flail*
Swither, *between two opinions, dilemma*
Syne, *afterwards, next*

## T.

Taks, *takes*
Tammocks, *hillocks*
Tapt, *knock'd gently*

Tarrow'd, *loathed*
Tates, *small parcels*
Tents, *listens, observes, marks*
Thiggin, *a polite way of begging*
Thule, *one of the Hebrides*
Timmer spurtles, *pieces of wood*
Tine, *lose*
Tips, *rams*
Titta, *sister*
Tod, *fox*
Toom, *empty*
Tweelie, *quarrel, battle*

## U.

Unco's, *strange stories, news*
Unken'd, *unknown, forget*

## W.

Waft, *woof*
Wa'fu', *woeful*
Waly, *a small flower*
Wa's, *walls*
Wauble, *to move up and down*
Weans, *children*
Wee wheen, *a small parcel*
Wha, *who*
Whamble, *tumble*
Whins, *furze*
Whups, *carries off suddenly*
Winsome, *cheerful, agreeable*

## Y.

Yaupish, *greedily*
Yeard, *earth*
Yotlins, *yellow-ammers*
Yowe, *ewe*

# ERRATA.

Page 3, line 1, for *learn*, read *practise*.—Ditto l. 10, for *hallow*, r. *hollow*.—P. 5, l. 2, and 4, for *a*, r. *a'*.—P. 10, end of l. 7, dele .—l. 16, r. *cleads*.—P. 14, l. 7, for *ne'er*, r. *nor*.—P. 17, l. 3, for *these*, r. *those*.—P. 19, l. 7, r. *as he, nane there was ever ken'd*.—P. 45, l. 6, for *a*, r. *an'*.—P. 46, l. 1, for *reign*, r. *rein*.—P. 57, l. 4, r. *unweildy*.—P. 63, l. 14, at the end put .—P. 70, l. 4, for *bills*, r. *fells*.—P. 72, l. 6, for *jumkin*, r. *jumpin*.—P. 78, l. 8, for *her*, r. *wi'r*.—P. 95, l. 16, r. *straightway*.—P. 113, l. 2, for *a'*, r. *o'*.—P. 133, l. 9, r. *bid*.—P. 173, l. 4, r. *seasons'*.—P. 176, l. 3, r. *through*.

www.ingramcontent.com/pod-product-compliance
Lightning Source LLC
Chambersburg PA
CBHW032130160426

43197CB00008B/586